To Clare —
My (tor)mentor, collegue and
Friend —
Enjoy The "ride"

The Chosen Path

By
Steven Damsker

Published by:
Steven Damsker

ISBN: 979-8-218-07317-6

Copyright ©2022

Cover Design & Interior Layout:
Bryan K Reed, www.bryankreed.com

Printed in the United States

Table of Contents

Life Begins 5
Adolescence 7
Semi-Maturity 11
Identity Crisis 13
Directional Challenges 17
Untying Apron Strings 19
New Surroundings 23
Self-Reflections 27
The History is Past (like hell) 31
A New Lease on Life 35
Road Warrior 39
Scary Times 45
Time for a Cold One 47
The Wind of War 49
You had a bad day 51
Game Changer 53
You Cannot Go Home Again 57
So Much Fun – So Little Time 61
Making a Life 63
Sun Fun 67
Jaw Drop Time 71
In Loving Memory 75
Epiphany 77
Mixed Blessings 81
Job Progression 85
California Dreaming 89
Mr. Nice Guy is an Oxymoron 91
Reality Wake-Up Call 93
And the Hits Keep Coming 95
Separation Anxiety or What Comes Around Goes Around 97
Breaking Up is (Not Always) Hard to Do 99
Changing Diapers and Changing Stripes 101
The Low Country 105
Children 107
The Brutal Truth 115
Movin' On Out 119
Deja Vous 121
Fairness 123
The End of the Corporate Risk Control Road 127
Changing Stripes, Again 131
Reality 135
Keep Climbing 137
A (not so) Lucky Break 143
Wedding Time 147
Turning a Corner 149
Wedding Part Deux 151
Living with Fear 153

Dedication

On September 12, 2018, dozens of natural gas explosions rocked three communities near Boston, MA, killing at least one person, injuring 12, and prompting the evacuation of hundreds of people. Upon learning this news, I called and explained to my older daughter, who resides in the greater Boston area with her family, that my first post-college job, in 1970, was working as a gas-leak detection consultant to find such leaks before tragedy struck. Her terse reply "How did I never know this about you?".

Hence, the idea for a memoir was formed.. This autobiography describes the joys, challenges, and rewards that most career-oriented people face; however, from my perspective, my career was a rollercoaster ride of thrills and surprises. This book was written with love as well as for all those who just like to laugh! Is dedicated to my wife Linda for her love and devotion and to our daughters Melanie Camp, son-in-law Matt, Amy Lynne Damsker/Wright, and son-in-law Glenn.

The stories within these pages relate the fun and excitement of raising children while also taking a cynical look at the real world of a career. For all who have been there/done that, enjoy the experience again. This roller-coaster will provide the thrills built up over a lifetime. Buckle-up and enjoy the ride!

1
LIFE BEGINS

During the approximate 9- month human gestation term our life's plan is created from our ancestral DNA. In the darkness of the womb our tactile senses and neuro-muscular activity emboldens us. We all then arrive in the same manner- naked, wet, and afraid. The first sensation of nuzzling, being tightly swaddled and nurtured in a care-free and loving environment, transforms us to our launching pad. From here on, what we feel, think, and do, along with genetics, will make us who we are.

Our first memories are fuzzy, meret flashes of what and where occasionally come to mind. The "when" hasn't formed yet as we don't develop the complex understanding of time until much later in development. The mobile on the crib, hugging the stuffed toy or standing in the crib and downing nature's nourishment may come to mind. It does to me. How do we know what we did back then? We have photos, stories, artifacts, and remember sounds or smells. There was no right from wrong but just the chance to grow like a delicate flower.

My father, Martin Udell, born 1909 in Brooklyn, NY. He was the second of seven children to Max and Rebecca ("Becky") Yudell (at some point he dropped the "Y"). In 1935 he married the love of his life, the 20 year old Rhoda Rich, also born in Brooklyn, NY.

Rhoda was the second of three daughters to Harry & Sylvia Rich. Martin ("Marty") earned a living as a men's clothing salesperson. He joined the US Navy in 1941 and valiantly served as an electrician's mate aboard a US Destroyer Escort in the perilous warzones of the Pacific Ocean. He was honorably discharged at the end of WW2 in 1945. After transitioning back to civilian life, they moved into a small Brooklyn apartment and let nature take over.

 I, Steven S. Udell, arrived at the world at 11:57pm on February 23, 1947, at Brooklyn NY's Beth-El hospital during a record NYC blizzard. I was born into a loving and large extended family with many aunts, uncles, and cousins on both sides. Early life indeed was good – until a life-changing event manifested just shy of my fourth birthday.

 My father, Martin, had been suffering from a skin ailment which was finally accurately diagnosed as a skin disease -"Exfoliative Dermatitis" - which was thought to be caused due to repeated exposure to natural rubber products utilized on the Navy vessel on which he was an electrician's mate. Treatments with traditional remedies were applied without success. A new drug, a steroid called cortisone, was applied to halt the progression of the disease; however, proper dosage back then was yet unproven and on Oct. 5, 1950, such efforts failed, and his life ended at age 41! Doctors had told me over my formative years that this was not a genetic trait and that I was "safe," although the worry has always remained.

2
ADOLESCENCE

Animals abandon their offspring as their young instincts take over. With humans, the bond continues much longer. Although family members may less like or appreciate each other over time, they are usually still there for the long term. My mother Rhoda's two married sisters, Lydia (2-years older) and Shirley (2-years younger) brought my newly widowed mother and me to live in their respective homes in Brooklyn over the next 3 years. Lydia's husband, Alexander, was a prominent psychiatrist. Shirley's husband, Joe, owned and operated a greenhouse and supplied businesses with various plants and floral arrangements. The wives all tended to the raising of my cousins and me.

I must digress here a bit as I cannot fail to mention, much less pay homage to my maternal and paternal grandparents. Everyone who remembers theirs holds memories of a special connection that remains regardless of when they passed. My maternal grandparents, Harry & Sylvia Rich, brought mom and me to live in Miami Beach, FL during the winter months at their rented quarters in the Mantel Plaza Arms - an apartment/hotel that is still standing (now a condominium), in the swanky Art-Deco South Beach area.

My grandpa Harry ("gramps") took me to see the TV idols of most young boys in the 1950s. We saw the Cisco Kid and Pancho, Hop-A- Long Cassidy and other famous cowboy stars of the black & white TV screen perform in outdoor arenas and darned if those dazzling outfits did not look cool. I also vividly recall being with him as we walked along the wide-open South Miami Beach strand where he would show and teach me all about the wide variety of seashells that washed ashore. I can still hear the "roar of the ocean" when holding a large conch shell to my ear – a fallacy not realized until many years later that it was simply my hearing the sound of air. Bummer!

My grandmother ("nana") was just a big bowl of love. She was a full-figured woman who would wrap around me and squeeze all but my last breath out of me all the while laughing and kissing me as "gramps" looked on. She was also an impressive cook that apparently neither knew nor cared anything about fats and calories. There was no "food police" back then and I can still smell the egg and flour blintzes frying in the butter and tasting the pot cheese filling. A burnt tongue was an insignificant sacrifice, but it was quickly cooled and quelled by the chilled sour cream! Mmmmmmmmmmmm!

My paternal grandparents, Max & Rebecca ("Becky") were European born around the late 1880s. and immigrated to the US through Ellis Island. They married here, and settled into an apartment along Brooklyn's Coney Island Avenue. They had seven children. As a child, I had fun trying to remember who lived where around the US. I do not recall Max's profession but as with all grandparents they doted on me and all my cousins.

In 1954, mom decided we had enough "schlepping" between Brooklyn and Miami Beach and opted to stay in FL, so she got a job as a secretary and moved us into an apartment in the Prince Michael Hotel in Miami Beach. I was turning seven. Because I had missed the age cutoff for Kindergarten in FL, I was enrolled in the first grade at North Beach elementary school. I even rode the public bus. Amazing right? Impossible today at that early age I suppose! What a life!?

North Beach Elementary is located on what was 41st Street in Miami Beach, FL. In the late 1940s and 1950s there was no bigger American media star than Arthur Godfrey, who had become known and loved for his intimate, folksy radio personality and went on to host programs like the wildly popular daily CBS variety show Arthur Godfrey Time. Beginning in 1953 Godfrey broadcast the show from the glitzy Kenilworth hotel. His star power brought business and tourism to burgeoning Miami Beach and for his contribution, 41st Street was co-named Arthur Godfrey Road.

Today, many years after the broadcaster put the city on the map his name all but vanished as the city's Neighborhood and Community Affairs committee voted unanimously to strip the popular broadcaster's name from the co-named 41st Street in a decades-old effort to rid Godfrey's name from one of the defining thoroughfares of the city. The commissioner calling for the change says he is not relevant anymore; others; however, allege he was anti-Semitic because of his partial ownership in a hotel with restrictive policies against Jews.

After two short years, everything in life is short when one is under 10 years of age, mom decided she had enough of the sun, so we relocated back to Brooklyn and moved into a little studio apartment on the third floor at 850 East 17th

Street and I was enrolled into the third grade at Brooklyn's elementary Public School 152. That school, built in 1906, still stands and is now a middle school. With mom busy working as a bookkeeper, my aunt Shirley took me to school that first day and I recall meeting my teacher. She reminded me of the wicked witch from the Wizard of Oz. She had a long-pointed nose, long spindly fingers and her voice crackled. She was indeed the source of nightmares. Mom had come to school a few days later to meet the teacher and I will never forget the surprised look on both her and the teacher's faces. The teacher, Ms. Provost, said "Hello Rhoda. How have you been?" Mom suddenly realized that Ms. Provost was also HER 3rd. grade teacher! Sometime later, mom admitted to me that Ms. Provost struck fear into her as well.

My maternal grandparents moved back to Brooklyn soon after mom and I did. They moved into what seemed like an impossibly huge apartment on Beverly Road which was three NYC subway stops from Avenue H on the BMT. Just as it was hard to believe that I rode the public bus to school in Florida, I rode the subway (above ground tracks in this part of the city) to Beverly Road. Mom would give me a subway token (a token cost 15 c) and Nana or Gramps would be waiting (no cell phones of course back then) to bring me to their apartment. This was my home away from home. I had plenty of toys there and Nana spoiled me rotten with all that (unhealthy) food that Jews devoured with gusto.

3
SEMI-MATURITY

In grades K-6 kids learn a lot about themselves. They do not know or understand why, it just is. I think that boys, such was I, learn right from wrong based on what they fear most. Bullying in elementary school is a rite of passage and there were those times where I know I hid in fear from some of the boys, but eventually I learned the value of pride.

At some point I had decided that shrinking away rather than holding my ground was not who I was or wanted to be. Of course, that kind of bravado can be a hard lesson. Then it happened. I do not know why boys think taunting is fun but following a school dismissal, two classmates decided that it was necessary for them to "have" my new jacket. After some well-placed kicks and punches at me to achieve their goal, I fought back and retreated WITH my jacket although not without a bloody nose and torn pants. I was now more in fear of what mom would say when I got home. She instinctively knew that I was growing up and other than a sympathetic hug and application of a washcloth (but thankfully without the anticipated scolding based on what had happened or a call to the school to complain) the incident passed without further ado. Thanks mom!

Years later I tried to instill the value of self-respect onto my young girls such that they too would stand up for their own self-respect when other kids displayed character flaws resulting in upsets and/or some hurt feelings. Whereas I never encouraged them to get physical to defend their honor I was shocked and sometimes amazed to see the differences in them in such matters. Where did one child learn defensive strategy (and apply it!) at such an early age and the other one shy away from such conflicts and simply come home and brood about it? Suffice to say and without embarrassment to either of them, they both grew up proud and strong (but damned-sure under the watchful eye of one who never accepted anything less).

4
IDENTITY CRISIS

In 1958 I turned eleven. My mother married Jules (Julie) Leon Damsker. Julie was a widower and lived in Brooklyn's East NY neighborhood. He was introduced to mom via a mutual friend while mom and I still lived on E. 17th Street in Flatbush. Julie was a union laborer (a commercial plumber) with plumbing union Local 1. He was a dashing and handsome man, not unlike the movie stars of the 1940s. He adored my mother and treated me with kindness. He had two children living with him – a son, 21 and a daughter, 16. On March 30, 1958, with many relatives present in my Aunt Shirley's living room, all witnessed the signing of the Ketubah - the Jewish prenuptial agreement considered an integral part of a traditional Jewish marriage, and outlines the rights and responsibilities of the groom, in relation to the bride. In modern practice, the Ketubah has no agreed monetary value, and is never enforced (except in Israel) and the marital ceremony included the Jewish tradition of the breaking of the glass. Soon after the wedding with another stroke of a pen at the office of a Family Court magistrate, Steven S. Udell was now Steven S. Damsker via the adoption process by Jules Damsker. I gained a new dad, two siblings, and a new name.

There are neither words nor feelings that could have come close to expressing how my life was suddenly transformed. I was now a kid-brother and one who now had the backing of a father-figure of a man that could do what no mother could in rearing an 11-year-old son. In short, he was an extraordinary man whom I admired. Although there were many wonderful experiences with my new stepdad, there was one that I fondly recall. In 1959 he took me to Yankee Stadium to see an exhibition game between the Yankees and the (recently moved to Los Angeles) Dodgers. Julie got us passes to box seats near the dugout.

WOWEE!! Go ahead. Take in that moment. Hear the roar, smell the fresh cut natural green-grass field, taste the hot dogs, and marvel at the grandeur of the "House that Ruth Built" that was constructed 1922 to 1923 for $2.4 million ($33.5 million in 2018 dollars). As we watched batting practice, a batted baseball rolled toward the base of the stands. Julie, never one to pass on an opportunity, opened the gate, walked onto the edge of the field, picked up and handed me that ball. I slept with that ball for weeks and forged Mickey Mantle's signature on it. Life was good!

As a new family unit, we moved into the upper floor of a two-family home on Brooklyn's East 92nd Street in the East NY neighborhood. My brother, Marty, had just completed his enlistment tour of duty with the US Navy and was now working on Wall Street. My sister, Susan, was a popular cheerleader at Tilden High. Yes, we were one big happy family - for a while.

Whereas I was thrilled to have a new family, I could sense some friction. My mother was always a stern, independent woman that liked doing things her way. Compromises were rare and differences of opinions and/or values were inevitable.

Being a stepmom to a 16 year old girl whose natural mother had passed away a few years prior, was difficult. Julie did his best to "calm the waters," but arguing with my mother was not in his best interest - or desire. Eventually, my sister's relationship with them reached its limit and after some heated spats she moved into an apartment with Julie's sister and as quick as it started it seemed that this new sibling relationship would vanish. My brother, Marty, hung back a while longer until he met the woman who would be his wife. They were married in 1963 and moved into a home in Mill Basin, Brooklyn.

In 1962, mom, Julie & I relocated back to 850 E. 17th Street into a 2-bedroom apartment on the sixth floor. I do not remember why we moved (smaller space, less rent I assume) but the move caused me to transfer during my sophomore year at Samuel J. Tilden to Midwood High School.

A transition at that age is hard, to say the least. One day in the Midwood cafeteria I was approached by a boy who I vaguely remembered from my time at PS 152. He jogged my memory as one of the boys from that earlier described "jacket incident." He remembered me and wasted no time to "shake me down" by demanding I hand over my lunch money. He was also looking to get even.

As can be imagined, that old memory of a schoolyard fight came into sharp focus. Now, truth be told I was never one to start fights and where or when possible, I simply did my best to avoid them. This "bully" as I was told later, had a bad reputation as a troublemaker. His problem though was that some years had passed since that schoolyard issue and now

I was about four inches taller than him and several pounds heavier. He was too dense to notice this difference but the laws of physics plus my memory suddenly came into play and his aggressive behavior ended when the law of gravity beckoned him onto the cafeteria floor when I pushed him away.

I kept my lunch money, and he got the "message." I had to sit in detention class for doing this, but I thought it was worth it as he never bothered me again. Was I proud of what I did? Damn right! My parents were told of my behavior. Mom scolded me. Julie, a rough and tumble union man, and no stranger to physical altercations, laughed and said, "Atta boy, kiddo." I knew he was proud of me. Mom, not so much but she never said anything further.

5
DIRECTIONAL CHALLENGES

Early one afternoon I was walking home from classes at Midwood. The distance home was about a mile and a half and part of the walk followed Campus Road around the football field of Brooklyn College. It was normal to see kids spending time together or leaning on parked cars to chat. What I came across was different. A car's radio was broadcasting some news and there were girls crying. It was about 2:00 PM on November 22, 1963. John Fitzgerald Kennedy had just been assassinated in Dallas, Texas.

In the middle of my HS junior year, I was at best a "C" student with a lack of direction and motivation. I was getting really scared because my future was in doubt. I knew I was not going to follow in the footsteps of cousins and friends that would be admitted to top colleges and then likely go onto rewarding, professional careers. I just was not wired that way. Trade schools were not the answer either as the stigma of a nice Jewish boy learning to be an air conditioning mechanic to me was a blasphemous notion. There was little time left before I would be done with high school and then what?

In 1963 at a family gathering, my mother's first cousin George, a pediatrician, talked with me about my future. He used to medically tend to all of us cousins as a sort of family doc so there was a special kinship there.

Cousin George was indeed as wise and he knew that I had a

penchant for science, but he also knew I did not have the grades for medical school. He looked at me knowing my interests in life sciences said one word: "agriculture"! Huh? What, farming? He said "no, research"! There is a need for an increased food supply and since research for growing crops is a science, I would do well to pursue a degree in agriculture. I had nothing else in mind and had little options so took a chance and applied to the State University of NY (SUNY) Agricultural & Technical College at Cobleskill, NY to major in Agronomy. I was accepted!!!

Sadly, Cousin George succumbed to brain cancer several years later, but his wisdom changed my life.

SUNY-Cobleskill's campus is nestled in a valley 140 miles north of NYC and forty miles west of Albany in Schoharie County. When I enrolled, it was a 2-year college, and the thinking was if I showed good academic progress I could apply to and transfer to a 4-year college and pursue the coveted BS degree. Was this all really my idea? Of course, not - but the indignity of a young Jewish kid not attending college was just too much to bear. What was I to do?

Gleefully, I was enrolled in the fall of 1964 and happy to be going to college! This academic institution today is a four-year university. Going off to college is an experience that crosses so many boundaries. Being on one's own away from direct parental supervision is itself an education. Academic and social aspects without direct parental supervision (or rebuke) really add to a person's character development, independence, and maturity. Responsibility becomes apparent and consequences are the best teachers. I had the time of my life and I also managed to get good grades.

6
UNTYING APRON STRINGS

At age 17, my first year at SUNY-Cobleskill, I resided in a Cape Cod-style rooming house a mile off-campus at 16 MacArthur Avenue. That building is still there today! As with a typical Cape Cod style house there were two upstairs bedrooms. My roommate, Ed, was from a suburb of Rochester NY (a city kid like me) who also selected the Agronomy major. Two boys shared the other room straight off their parent's upstate NY dairy farms. They were nice boys but without "city street smarts," and Ed & I had many laughs at their naivety.

To let off steam and have some good-natured adolescent fun we would all tag-team wrestle upstairs. The house mom, a large framed buxom woman (who occasionally baked us awesome cookies), would yell up and scold us because we were making a racket. That wood frame house must have felt like an earthquake the way we let off steam. The house dad, a home furnace technician, would come home after work in his oil and ash-stained coveralls, wheezing from the soot and his unfiltered Camel cigarettes. After being told of our ruckus, he threatened to throw us out if we do not cut it out. We never took him seriously. We should have.

Ed had one of those immersion coil heaters. Put the metal coil into a bowl of soup mix with water; plug it in and in a minute, hot soup! Trouble was, as we soon learned, 15 amp fuses could not manage the power surge if anything else was plugged into the same circuit and turned on. If a clock radio were on, and we plugged in the heating coil, the fuse would blow. But Ed and I were resourceful (and street-smart, remember?) so we bought a box of fuses and when no one was home, we would replace the fuse and all was "A-ok" (US Air Force Lt. Col. John "Shorty" Powers popularized the expression "A-ok" while NASA's public affairs officer for Project Mercury, and attributed to astronaut Alan Shepard during his Freedom 7 Mercury-Redstone 3 first USA human spaceflight, on May 5, 1961. The objective was to put an astronaut into orbit around the Earth and return him safely).

So, early one morning (following another batch of scolding and threats of evictions due to our horseplay the day before) we awoke for class to the sound of the house dad's electric razor in their downstairs bathroom. It was also pitch dark outside and colder than you know what! So, yes, we did.

Silence reigned and inside darkness loomed. The house dad was heard stumbling in the dark and with a flashlight he found the fuse box and replaced the fuse himself with his spares. We repeated this little game on and off for a few days, but the house dad got wind of it and said he wanted us out by the next day. He knew that Ed & I were the instigators and thus he let the other two off the hook. So, we called and took refuge at the school Dean's house and slept on the floor of his living room that Friday night. From there I called Julie. In a flash on Saturday morning, he drove the 3-hours up (without mom) in his 1962 Buick LeSabre and we all, including the Dean, met at the rooming house where Julie made the peace

– one laborer to another. Afterward, Julie quietly laughed at the whole episode but sternly told us to cut it out, which we did when returned to our room in the house and behaved.

  Sort of.

7
NEW SURROUNDINGS

The campus at SUNY-Cobleskill in 1964 consisted of four buildings arranged in a quadrangle - "The Quad" - atop a hill overlooking a ski valley. The scenery was spectacular all year long, but the winters were indeed a sight to see. Snow was measured by the foot and walking up that hill from the rooming house to classes was indeed a chore. Physical education was part of every curriculum. So, with that much snow and a big hill, skiing was a natural choice for recreation!

The ski instructor was a WW2 combat soldier in France as a member of the famed US Army Ski Patrol. He was a real hero! We were all outfitted with ill-fitting US Army surplus ski boots and skis, ski poles, and with our eyes wide open (behind clunky goggles), we stepped over the edge and learned how to overcome fear as we blasted off into never-never land while screaming our heads off.

Of course, within like 10 seconds most of us were human snowballs aimlessly careening down the slope tumbling over our butts in a whiteout. I recall that "note-to-self" moment - this is extremely dangerous! So much for logic as we trudged up and repeated the process until each made it down standing.

For the start of the 1965 fall term, I moved to the men's dorm. Although there was no escaping the trudging through the eventual deep snow to reach classes, the dorm life was a hoot. It was a rush for all the guys there (note: coed dorms were not until many years later in society). Yes, we studied, but man-oh-man did we ever party.

Back "then" the legal drinking age in New York State was eighteen. I turned eighteen on Feb. 23, 1965, so drinking for me was now actually legal. Not that that would have stopped me before, but it certainly made beer purchases easier! Welcome to rite-of-passage number one.

We all of course knew nothing of alcoholic quality, and many of us learned the hard way that Sloe Gin and Port Wine make for an awful and sickening time later. We also learned that Seagram's 7 was much better, and we would all chip in to buy it along with bottles of 7-Up to create the classic cocktail mix called 7&7 (of course you recall that, right?).

Turning eighteen also led to rite-of-passage number two - obtaining a New York State driver's license. Upstate NY and New Jersey kids got theirs at 17. Not NYC kids! The NYC law was eighteen! To get a license, I had to take a road test. To do this, I needed to have a car. Thankfully, my old housemates from the McArthur Avenue house stepped up and made sure I learned how to drive on snow and ice, which was everywhere up there from November to May. So, on a Sunday morning while stores were still closed, they drove me to a snow and ice-covered IGA Supermarket and shopping plaza parking lot and proceeded to teach me how to drive in the winter.

Let me tell you, a 1960 Chevrolet Bel Air was one beast of a car. It had a long wheelbase, huge tale-fins, no seatbelts (not yet a law), no anti-lock brakes or radial tires (neither were yet available), ran on leaded gasoline, got 15 MPG and it had a lot of power. I was handed the keys as I sat behind the wheel as the others moved over. I was imagining I was on the launch pad on Cape Kennedy (since renamed back to Cape Canaveral) for a NASA Apollo mission.

Following my "learned" colleague's instruction, I placed my right foot on the break, started the engine, pulled the gearshift on the steering column forward and lowered it from park to drive. With nothing at all except the light snow and ice-covered pavement ahead I let my foot off the brake and as the car began creeping forward in gear, placed it on the accelerator. It was now "show-time." I was instructed to "take it up" to about 20 mph and then slam on the brakes. I did wheelies, donuts, skids, etc. No one was injured nor was anything damaged as a result. They were great guys, and it was a great car! What fun! What idiots! Two weeks later, with the same car for the official road test in Schoharie County NY, I passed written and road tests and soon I was in possession of my first driver's license.

As stated, the new experiences at college were great, but not always. Upstate NY was quite different from the urban life in NYC, and it was not populated by a wide variety of open-minded individuals. A sinister experience slowly began to emerge and one day it surfaced in its true form: Antisemitism!

Although it was nowhere near the level of this bigoted form of racism experienced by the older generation, it was indeed new to me and very upsetting. Jokes and pranks are usually fine but personal attacks cross a line. One afternoon upon returning to my dorm room I noted that one of the 3x5 index cards in the metal sleeve on the door that showed my name was adorned, no, defaced! with capital "J"'s around my name. Yes, I can take a joke, but this was NOT funny.

I had an inkling as to who were the culprits and later that day, I stated my disapproval of their prank and asked that they not repeat it. Later that evening several of us, including these so called 'friends" went to unwind at a local bar. One of the guys went to the bar to get a drink and yelled across the floor, "Hey Jew boy, you want a beer?" I nodded yes and when he placed the bottle on the table I stood up and cold-cocked him and before he could react. He stopped, realized his so-called humor truly was not a smart move and apologized. Diplomacy? Perhaps not, but it did not happen again.

Later, I explained that actions have consequences. Although, I knew he was simply just not aware of how offensive his actions were, including the door defacing, which he later admitted to. It was stuff like that could also get his ass kicked out of school.

8
SELF-REFLECTIONS

After getting my driver's license, I really wanted my own wheels. What young kid does not? My dorm roommate was also from Rochester, NY. His family owned and lived on a small farm. He said they have an old 1960 Renault Dauphine that I can have for $50! I asked Julie, knowing what mom would have said, and he not only sent me the money to buy it but added it onto the family auto insurance policy too! When we went to get it, I had a slight problem in that I had no idea how to operate a manual shift transmission. After a little practice I got the hang of it and drove it back to school.

The French may know how to make wine and are great cooks but cars? Forget it! The car had all the power of a manually operated eggbeater and if it was going downhill with a tail wind, I was barely able to keep up in traffic. Did I care? Heck no. I had a car!!!!!

Some months later I drove the Renault home to Brooklyn for a long weekend. I was excited to go home but for another reason. I was "sweet" on a young lady from high school, and we had started dating before I left for college. We kept up the relationship via talking long distance on payphones and I paid in cash with a pocketful of change into the phone's coin box (no cell phones yet). We also wrote letters back and forth often (no emails back then either). For all of these reasons plus the long distance, I was eager to see her.

The Renault, (again, the French made a crappy car) was never rust-proofed and the chassis fell apart to the point it was too dangerous to operate. Good-bye car. My girlfriend also turned out to be unfaithful and when I learned that all along, she was dating one of my friends, it was good-bye girlfriend.

During this year, I was thinking about what the relationship with my sister that was essentially "ended" when there was that "parental rift." I had learned from my brother that she got married over a year ago in a NYC civil ceremony via a Justice of the Peace and she and her husband and their new baby daughter along with their pet Schnauzer lived in a studio apartment on Ocean Avenue near E. 17th Street. I wrote her a letter, and we re-kindled, in secret from the parents. That reconnection was nice.

In the spring of 1966, I received my Associate in Applied Science (AAS) degree in Agronomy. I had even made the Dean's list. Was the course work difficult? Not as I recall but I do know that I found it far more interesting than what I was supposed to learn back in high school. So now what? Pursuit of the BS degree was the next challenge and so I applied and again was thrilled to be accepted into the Agronomy curriculum at North Carolina State University at Raleigh NC.

Over the summer of 1966 following graduation from SUNY-Cobleskill I got a job with the NYC Health & Hospital Corp. My Uncle Al had "connections" and I was hired as a driver of service vehicles but was also trained as an ambulance driver. Seriously! That is until my uncle heard about it and then had me transferred to the pest control department where I drove a truck from Manhattan, and via the Staten Island ferry, to Staten Island where guys in the truck bed would spray highly toxic mosquito abatement chemicals in residential areas. Local kids would all run into the fog laughing. Today those chemicals are banned today.

Once more I was reassigned to pick up and shuttle doctors all over Manhattan to various hospitals for meetings. The cars were also equipped with flashing red lights and a siren. To switch from horn to siren there was a toggle switch on the dashboard. I did not notice that a driver before me must have engaged the siren mode and left it as is. While on East River Drive, I wanted to get past a slow-moving vehicle and in doing so, I "beeped" the horn. The siren wailed and the lights flashed. It scared the heck out of me and almost sent the slower car into the river.

After that, I was sure that I learned how to maneuver in NYC traffic better than a NYC cabbie. A skill that also came in handy after college - which I will explain later.

9
THE HISTORY IS PAST (LIKE HELL)

In the fall of 1966, I enrolled at NC State. I lost a year of college credits on this transfer, but I was here and that is all that mattered. That is until some of the classes I had to take were more of a challenge than I expected. My math aptitude at the REAL college level was bad. English classes were equally tough, especially since the professors were biased against "Yankees" and were, to my mind, unfair with the grading of essays. I muddled through with a "C" average and attended summer school to shore up the GPA.

The "fun" classes were chemistry, biology, zoology, botany, genetics, soil science, crop science and others more aligned with the major. Thus, my first year at a 4-yr university was underway and completed without too much difficulty.

Following the end of the 1968 fall semester, I needed a break and took off the spring semester to try working for a living and got a job with the NC Water & Air Resources department as a field technician. My job was to drive a NC government pick-up truck and take water samples from NC waterways before and after industrial sites utilized the waters. All NC waterways were classified as A, B or C for water quality and downstream samples had to be no worse than the upstream supply or the industrial site utilizing the water would face heavy fines in accordance with the Federal and State's Clean Water Act.

So, I was the "gofer" that pulled up water samples from highway bridges and from often hard to find culverts. I evaluated the samples for pH, nitrogen level, coliform bacteria, biological oxygen demand (BOD), chemical oxygen demand (COD) and applied some preservative reagents. I then placed the samples in a cooler and drove back to the State offices, dropped the pick-up truck at the motor pool and brought the cooler to the lab upstairs then went back to my apartment.

Oh! I had also purchased a 1962 Ford Falcon for $300! It was a screaming machine (not).

One day, while taking samples in the mountainous western part of NC, there I was in boots, an old army surplus jacket and a state-issued machete to cut through the underbrush to get to the water. As I emerged from the underbrush onto a path with the sample jar in hand, three men in their thirties greeted me. They wore ball caps, flannel shirts and khaki pants. One was carrying a rifle across his chest. I assumed they were hunters. They asked what I was doing, and we exchanged some pleasantries.

I then headed to the pick-up truck for the long drive back to the lab. I thought nothing about this chance encounter until I got back to the lab and mentioned it to one of the lab techs. He and others that heard this looked at me and turned ashen. One said I was lucky to be alive. He said if in fact I was not such a "dumb Yankee," they would have suspected I knew that I had entered near their moonshine operation, and I would still be there – dead. OK lesson learned. The hits keep coming!

On another return to the motor pool garage and lab I needed a restroom ASAP, so I walked to the back of the garage and noted two prominent signs. White & Colored! Wow. I had heard of this but never saw it. Again, proving my ignorance I said to a mechanic about the size of "Haystacks" Calhoun (who was the famous gargantuan wrestler that drew crowds during the 1950s and 1960s, sporting his trademark white T-shirt, blue overalls, and horseshoe necklace) that I thought racially segregated restrooms were outlawed by the 1964 Civil Rights Act.

Well, ole "Haystacks" pounded the palm of his hand with a torque wrench about the size of my leg and through a tobacco-stained beard and yellowed teeth he grinned at me and in perfect southern diction said, "well college boy, yawls in the south and yawl's hasta learn." Thankfully, that was all that happened. I no longer wondered why I did not do well in that first-year English class.

10
A NEW LEASE ON LIFE

I re-enrolled at NC State for the 1969 spring semester. I was twenty-two! That year was filled with turmoil as the Viet-Nam conflict was on everyone's mind. The US military draft at that time was based on a lottery system. 366 blue plastic capsules that contained the birthdays were chosen in the first draft lottery drawing on December 1, 1969. The first birth date drawn that night assigned as number 001 was September.

All males over eighteen born on Feb 23 just so happened to be assigned number 57 - meaning they were more likely to be drafted. I thought I was "safe" from the draft since I was a full-time student, but that changed quickly when I had dropped a class and my schedule was reduced from twelve down to nine credits. I may as well have waived a red flag at a bull as within a noticeably brief time I received the feared "Greetings" letter from the Brooklyn NY office of the US Selective Service Commission to report for a physical and subsequent Army induction.

I succeeded in delaying this by transferring the draft board to Raleigh, NC since I was paying rent and taxes (on my car) and was registered to vote. Nice try. Somehow, they too knew my credit status dropped below the full-time student deferment minimum, and a few weeks later I received another "Greetings" letter and was "invited" to report to the Raleigh, NC induction facility for the US Army.

As a kid in Brooklyn, I used to visit a podiatrist to routinely remove excess callous and deep, painful corns caused by "high arches." This condition in medical parlance is known as Pes Caves. So, armed with a copy of this medical record, I arrived at the induction center to report for the mental and physical exam.

I quickly surmised that the physical portion of the exam was the ability to "walk down the hall" and the mental portion was the understanding of the directional command to "Turn left." Thankfully, a clerk reviewed the medical record I had provided and decided that I needed to be evaluated by a specialist at the Fort Bragg Army base (home of the famed US Army 101st Airborne Division) to determine my fitness for military service.

So, a week or so later I drove the approximate one hundred miles ever so slowly to Fort. Bragg, in Fayetteville, NC. I was ushered in to meet with a young Army doctor with the rank of Captain. He conducted a cursory exam of my feet and without even looking at the medical record I had submitted asked me the one question I shall never forget, " Do I want to join the Army?"

Before I could utter what, he knew would most assuredly be a "no" he said I have a condition known as Pes Caves and although this is not a serious condition, regulation issue army boots may make it worse, and Uncle Sam might have a financial obligation to treat me and/or provide me with corrective orthotics long into the future. He then said IF I PREFERRED, he would issue me a medical deferment and I would not be subject to the draft.

Although some guys might think that this was a coward's excuse, and I would not argue, I had no qualms with those that were willingly inducted, but I also saw it as my lawful choice of either entering a controversial and deadly jungle warfare or staying put. I opted for the latter. The drive back to Raleigh was as fast as my Ford Falcon would fly without falling apart. My housemate, Elliot, had, that same day, just passed his "orals" exam for his Master of Science degree. Everything from about 5:00 pm until about noon the following day was lost in a mutually enjoyed alcoholic fog. I was now free of the draft worry and rededicated myself to my studies.

The spring of 1969 marked my fifth year of college in pursuit of my BS degree. I had way more credits than needed to graduate but I still lacked a couple of what I (not they) considered to be useless math courses that were required for graduation. My plan was to gain employment at the USDA's research facilities in Hyattsville, MD. I inquired and learned that if I qualified, the GS-4 level pay was pitifully low and did not include any travel reimbursement. No thanks! Luckily, there were job recruiters on campus seeking Ag major candidates. One recruiter represented Heath Consultants, Inc., a Boston area (Wellesley Hills) based consulting company offering a field job with travel and expenses!

It looked like it could be an interesting, purposeful, and rewarding opportunity. I spoke with the on-campus recruiter who approved me for an interview in Boston. I was sent an air ticket to Boston for the formal interview and was hired. They did not mind that I would not have my BS degree completed in time to start but they did encourage me to finish it as soon as I could. So, after racking up many miles on the old Falcon, I sold it for $150, borrowed parental money, upgraded to a used 1964 Buick Skylark and left NC State in the summer of 1969. I drove back to Brooklyn and hung out at "home" until I drove to Massachusetts in September to report for work with Heath Consultants, Inc. They secured lodging for me with other new recruits in a rooming house in Natick MA and my career was underway.

11
Road Warrior

My first full-time job! It sounds so trite and unimpressive, but it was neither. I accepted the job knowing that I was hired based on my agricultural education, but I learned soon enough that once hired, to just do what I was told and let the job steer me rather than vice-versa.

I was hired with the unflattering title of "Leak Detection Technician." Heath Consultants, Inc., formed in 1933, was contracted with municipal utility companies to survey underground gas and/or water mains to detect system leaks. Surveys inside municipal buildings were also conducted. Detecting underground gas main leaks simply required poking a hole in the ground with a plunger bar (a long spike with a sliding weight to drive it into the ground) near the identified gas line and using a probe attached to a combustible gas indicator meter, determine any leak and if found, measure the severity of the leak, mark it on a map and call it in to the utility for repair.

It was an easy job – in nice weather. In freezing rain sleet and snow, not so much. Remember this the next time you see utility workers in the freezing cold or sizzling summer heat and just nod a thank you.

Water main leak detection was also a challenge. To locate a leak, I wore large clunky headphones connected to a sonic detection probe attached to and powered by a heavy battery pack slung on my shoulder. I would touch the probe tip to fire hydrants to hear rushing water below ground. Trouble was that traffic noise impeded this testing, so it had to be done when there was no traffic, in the wee hours of the morning as well as in the rain or snow and bitter cold.

On occasion, I would conduct gas leakage surveys within municipal buildings. I would spray soap solutions on pipe joints and where bubbles occurred, there was a leak. In a maintenance utility garage, I was looking for the gas meter. I spotted it across the mezzanine and walked toward it when suddenly there I was, dangling ten feet off the concrete floor below being supported only by the fluorescent lighting wires that caught me between my legs when I fell through the ceiling tiles. Thankfully, I was quickly and gently rescued via ladder with the aid of workers. I was safe but walked a little funny for a while after.

After about a month of this work, the job - and my life - changed drastically. I was making money and paid my parents back for the car loan. I then traded in the Skylark and, via a bank loan, upgraded to a new 1970 Buick Opal. It was a fun sports car but a few weeks later during a weekend trip home to NY, it was totaled in an intersection. No injuries, but no car!

My employer, Heath Consultants, Inc. decided to send me on the road where I would drive company-supplied or rental vehicles and sometimes haul needed equipment in an attached trailer. I would collect my paycheck via General Delivery mail at a main post office at the next destination- if I were lucky. If I missed it, it was forwarded to the next location. Sometimes I was without a paycheck for over a month. Back then there were no credit or debit cards or ATMs. Checking accounts were available to open but they were branch specific. I had purchased traveler's checks and had to be cautious with my cash supply. This turned out to be good fiscal training!

I did the jobs called for via the agreements with the utility companies. I began road travel to conduct gas leakage surveys in Western PA, then Ohio and Michigan. It was all interesting work and at times the findings were a bit scary.

In Western PA there were many underground pockets of natural gas that filtered into abandoned coal mines. The problem was that there were homes built over these areas and now and then a gas pocket, developed from an old leaking cast iron gas main would seep into a basement and sometimes violently explode if the resident turned on a light switch.

Thus, my job had real relevance especially if I found the leakage first! The surveys in Western PA often required the use of an air compressor and a jack hammer to pierce through the frozen ground. The winter temperatures hovered near zero and the wind was fierce. Yes, the thought did occur to me, "What the hell am I doing here?"

I did the job a while longer and then moved onto the Cincinnati, OH area for more of the same. Early spring had arrived by then and working conditions were better. At that point anything was better than that work in PA. I collaborated with a partner in Cincinnati and stayed in a seedy motel in Covington, KY. All I will say is that it was "the other side of the tracks" but on my per diem allowance, it was what

I could afford. Following the Ohio work, I continued west onto the Detroit, MI metro area. OMG!

I was instructed to report to the gas company offices in Pontiac, MI, not too far from Detroit. Pontiac, the city named for an Odawa war chief known for his role in leading Native Americans in a struggle against British military occupation of the Great Lakes region, is also where General Motors manufactured the now defunct brand of Pontiac cars.

On arrival, I was advised that the local public utility's union called a strike and thus I would be accompanied by a young management supervisor in place of a union representative to travel with me and identify the suburban areas that needed to be surveyed. Now, the "normal" vehicle used to conduct these street surveys was the modified Ford Bronco which I had been driving. Attached to the front of the vehicle were two folding booms and each could be mechanically lowered such that the gas detection sensors would be lowered to just above the street level. As the vehicle was driven at a slow speed along the curb, the sensors would mechanically "sniff" for methane gas. Such would not be the case here as the powerful union would be quite agitated if they knew or worse, saw this was being done during their strike. Julie was not happy that I was "scabbing," but nothing further was said.

A contingency plan was hastily created by placing sensors just below the front bumper of a 1970 Chevy Chevelle with various gas sampling canisters in the trunk attached via tubes under the car to the sensors. Very James Bond!

So, the young supervisor and I set out to the area to be surveyed, and once there, I drove very slowly along the edges of the curbs of an upscale residential area. All was working OK until we entered a cul-de-sac. As we drove inward, I noted a large Chevy Suburban backing out of a driveway and beginning to block the exit out of the cul-de-sac. My young partner groaned and said, "Uh oh, that's the union's Vice President."

Great!

Here is that earlier reference to my driving prowess, honed on the streets of NYC. I glanced at my young assistant and said tighten that seat belt (thankfully now mandatory safety equipment in all US cars). I further said, "We're getting the hell out of here NOW!"

I yanked the steering wheel hard left and mashed the accelerator to the floor. The rear-wheel drive tires squealed, and we snuck past the Suburban with truly NO room to spare. I made a beeline to the interstate called the Wide Track for an escape to the gas company offices. To our surprise and horror, the Suburban followed and caught up to us on the Wide Track. We were in the right lane and the VP pulled alongside us in the center lane. With a menacing look he waved what looked like a pistol in our direction. True or not, that was enough for me. With no one close behind me I hit the brakes hard, and he flew past us.

I exited the Wide Track immediately and drove to the gas company offices where I picked up a phone and called Heath's office in MA, told them what just happened and that I wanted out of there ASAP. They obliged. As fate would have it, that union strike turned out to my advantage as I was directed to swap out the Chevelle for my old Ford Bronco leak plotter unit and drive out to Visalia California to conduct gas leakage surveys across open fields of high-pressure buried gas main transmission lines for Southern California Natural Gas. This was my opportunity to do an agricultural survey. I was excited.

What a trip! This was my first foray out west and once past the interstate routes through Michigan, Illinois, Missouri, and Oklahoma most of the way I followed the old legendary Route 66 through the Texas panhandle, into New Mexico, Arizona, and into California. I kept thinking about the 1960s TV show, Route 66 that followed two young men traversing the United States in a Chevrolet Corvette convertible, and the events and consequences surrounding their journeys. My Bronco was quite different from that Corvette, but the scenery was spectacular. I drove across the rim of the Painted Desert and saw part of the Grand Canyon. Indeed this "city kid" got to see the USA.

I was provided with this scope of work due to my education. The nature of the job was to slowly drive across large areas of farmland and look for necrotic changes in crops such as soybeans, lettuce, etc.

Where such areas were spotted, due to natural gas leaks from the buried high pressure distribution lines, I would follow up with the probe and measuring unit. I was pretty accurate. Findings were sent to the gas utility to begin repairs. High pressure leaks cost the utility money and needed to be repaired ASAP.

12
SCARY TIMES

Prior to 1973 when Motorola produced the first handheld mobile phone, the most common means of communication was the landline. I would check in with the office in MA daily (via collect calls of course) for any updates, job information, progress reports etc. Given the 3-hour time change I had to wait until after 9:00am EST to "call in".

The 1971 San Fernando earthquake, also known as the Sylmar earthquake, struck the San Fernando Valley near Sylmar at 6:55 a.m. PST on Feb. 9, 1971, with a magnitude of 6.6. The quake killed 66 people and caused horrific damage to infrastructure and properties. I was 2.5 hours north at the time of the quake and learned about it when I called my home office.

My job assignment was hastily changed and since we were still under contract with Southern California Natural Gas, I was instructed to drive down to LA and report to their offices in the San Fernando Valley ASAP. I do not recall how I found them or many of the other unimportant details but the next day there I was with SCNG crews trying to locate gas leaks even though the gas main systems were shut off.

I had badged authorized access to areas not even allowed to the local news crews. I wore a safety vest, steel-toe boots, a hard hat and safety glasses and I carried my sensing equipment. I vividly remember looking at the Olive View

Hospital. Three floors of the newly built six-story Olive View Hospital were "pancaked." There was a row of about 60 Los Angeles County ambulances which were all crushed by a collapsed parking overhang.

What went through my mind was that unlike a hurricane, which is radar-tracked, and warnings issued in advance, all earthquakes (including any aftershocks) happen with no warning and while on the scene of this tragedy it hit me that it can happen again like here and NOW. Thankfully, it did not.

Following this assignment, I took off a few days and visited cousins in Los Angeles, went to Disneyland and attended a Dodger's game at Dodger Stadium, sadly no foul ball this time.

13
Time for a Cold One

My next assignment took me to Northern California for contract work at the San Francisco Navy Yard and in surrounding towns. As with all other assignments, my evenings were my own and what better town was there to enjoy than San Francisco? Bars were on every block filled with rock music. Creedence Clearwater Revival cover bands and "flower power" people were everywhere, and some "interesting aromas" permeated the air. Meeting people was easy, and friendships were formed fast. We took in a San Francisco Giants baseball game at the old Candlestick Park. Back then it was OK to bring in your own beer. So, we brought in acase of Olympia beer and watched the game from the grandstand seats.

News flash: attending a baseball game in a stadium adjacent and open to the swirling winds from San Francisco Bay is akin to being placed in a meat locker. The beer helped numb the cold!

Routine gas leakage detection surveys followed in the Bay area for the next month or so. I was really enjoying the territory and inquired if there was any possibility of a permanent assignment out there. I knew that there was plenty of needed work available and I was getting a bit tired of living out of a suitcase and staying in cheap motels.

I was single, had no possessions beside my personal belongings and really wanted a growth opportunity in a place I would like to lay down roots. The answer came back as a definite maybe. I had the experience and there was an opening for a territory manager for Northern California business – but they needed me elsewhere for a while longer. I had obtained a nice new company issued van with an array of new equipment and was directed to drive up to Fairchild Air Force base near Spokane, WA for surveys.

The drive up through Northern California and Oregon was stunning. Beautiful mountains and scenic vistas are everywhere but I was ill-prepared for the travel experience.

14
THE WIND OF WAR

I had been driving for a while. It was getting late, and I was tired. So I stopped for a bite to eat and then proceeded to a local RV park near Bend, Oregon. I didn't need a water or power supply hook-up, so I simply made a bedroll with clothes and a coat and slept in the van. I awoke just before dawn and it was freezing. Ice coated the inside of the windows from my own breathing. I utilized the public shower facilities, did laundry, and then cranked up the van for heat.

Little did I know but I happened to be at an elevation of about 4,000 feet in the Cascade Mountains. The assignment was to drive the leak plotter over the natural gas piping buried under the air base's concrete aprons, taxiways, and runways. It began as a routine survey, but it was anything but that!

Fairchild Air Force Base was built for the military in 1942 and is home to the US Strategic Command's strategic deterrence missions. It is primarily an air-to-air refueling base and predominant aircraft was KC-135 air refueling tankers (the military version of the Boeing 707) and the almighty B-52 Superfortress capable of delivering nuclear bombs. The base spanned a lot of territory such that it would require several days to complete surveys with my slow-moving vehicle. Communications at a military base are, obviously, critical.

Each morning I was given maps of where to survey. Buried

gas lines; however, do not simply run in one direction. They also bisect taxiways and (active) runways. With clearance from the AF tower personnel, I began surveying across the tarmac following the map of the gas main layout and I began to diagonally cross a runway when my gas detection instrumentation suddenly pegged at the maximum levels. I had never had this happen but suddenly discovered why.

A KC-135 tanker was on final runway approach and sailed about five hundred feet over me, I did not see, hear, or feel it until it was well past me and then the jet wash almost blew my van and I off the ground. All was fine but I had to fill out some forms.

Ya think?

15
YOU HAD A BAD DAY

So, I was at a corrugated plant in the suburbs of the Windy City to conduct a routine safety tour for OSHA compliance as well as other general perils such as property protection and environmental concerns. Then it happened. Corrugated plants receive delivery of multi-ton paper rolls from the paper mills. The usual delivery mode is via rail cars backed into the plant adjacent to a concrete platform where lift trucks would unload the rolls. It's critical to avoid movement of the rail cars so a lift truck driver would place a heavy steel ramp and anchor it to both the rail car and the platform via steel pins. Then the paper off-loading may begin. When all paper rolls have been removed from the rail car, the platform anchors and the steel ramps are removed and the rail cars are pulled out of the plant.

Not today.

Someone forgot one platform ramp that remained anchored which caused the rail car to sway right and left as the engine began removing the rail cars. The sway to the right hit the platform then the inertia to the left hit the plant's outer concrete wall knocking out blocks and the roof support structure causing a partial collapse. I was in a safe area and heard the loud sounds of ensuing damage. All hell broke loose then I heard the sirens of the fire and EMS trucks. Thankfully no one was injured. As I went outside to assess the damage I noted a plant dumpster on the property. It was of ordinary waste but I noted "empty" paint cans as well as an open and dripping container of hydraulic oil. Ducky. Oh… the dumpster was placed over a sewer grate and leaking its liquid content into the sewer. That prompted a call to the State EPA.

With not much much more I could do I exited the property and headed to O'Hare airport for my flight home.

16
GAME CHANGER

Following the survey at Fairchild Air Force Base I was once again summoned back to the San Francisco area to conduct additional surveys in Burlingame and South San Francisco. All went according to plan and now I thought I would get the opportunity to get that coveted area manager job that was "hinted '' last time. The answer was yes…with one more delay. I was needed in Minneapolis/St. Paul for survey work with Minnesota Natural Gas.

I flew out of SFO on a beautiful 65°F sunny July day and landed at MSP amid one of the worst heat waves to hit the area in years. It was 103°F and with high humidity. San Francisco rarely has either condition.

The surveys were in Le Sueur country, home of the fabled Jolly Green Giant character associated with B&G Foods and the advertising title song made popular by those "Louie-Louie" guys, The Kingsmen. The legend of The Kingsmen's "Louie-Louie" has been told as many times as the song itself has been covered. The song's popularity among a new generation of rock-and-roll teenagers brought it to the attention of some concerned citizens. One of them, the father of a teen-age girl, wrote to Robert Kennedy, who was then the US Attorney General, to complain about the song's possible obscenity, prompting an F.B.I. investigation. "This land of ours is headed for an extreme state of moral degradation," the incensed parent wrote to Kennedy. (Remember this the next time someone tries reminiscing to you about the good old days before pop music was full of sex and vulgarities).

Once again, survey work was performed and again, I had a partner.

He had the vehicle needed for the surveys, so we worked together.

He was an interesting guy, a bit older, and had a constant urge for caffeine. We spent more time going for coffee than working. What happened next is one of the most hilarious episodes in my life.

It was getting near lunchtime, so we stopped at a local diner. He parked the leak plotter vehicle in front of the diner, and we went inside to order lunch. Within a few minutes an elderly couple that had just given the once-over of our vehicle parked out front. My partner saw them and in a whispered tone instructed me to not say a word. Sure enough, the couple approached our table and asked if that was our vehicle. My partner nodded in the affirmative. Then the older man asked the inevitable question, "What is it?"

Oh boy! I should have seen this coming. My partner politely pointed to the two empty chairs at our table and invited them to sit down, which they did with enormous curiosity. My partner opened his billfold and quickly flashed his company ID which to the uninformed looked eerily like a police or FBI badge. He said OK, we will tell you but request that you do not tell anyone about it. With their eyes and mouths wide open in anticipation, and nodding OK, my partner asked if they had heard of or read any of the stories about UFO sightings in the upper Midwest.

There was a very slow affirmative nod from both whence upon my partner said we work with a division of NASA, and we use that vehicle, he pointed to it out the window, to detect and gather very fine particulate matter that is believed to be not of this earth, and we then send it to a lab for further analysis. He then said this is all I can tell you, so again, please keep this talk private, OK? The couple nodded and slowly backed away with no expression, got up and walked out without ordering anything.

My partner then said to me "Wait ten minutes, as this isn't over yet." He was right.

To the minute a Minnesota State Patrol squad car quietly pulled up and parked next to our rig and two burly MSP officers walked in slowly. They looked in our direction and proceeded to our table. Without our invite as we did with the couple, they each pulled a chair out, turned it around, placed their massive forearms on the backs of their chairs and leaned in. The police officers looked at my partner and I and one of them in a calming, but assertive tone, said "OK fellas – you are scaring the locals. What are you doing with that vehicle?" This time the billfold came out and the ID was shown and explained. The police officers did not find humor in what we did, and "asked" that we not do it again and left.

A few days later I was informed that my company had filled that San Francisco Bay area manager's spot with someone more senior and that I would not have that job. I immediately pondered my future, and I reconsidered an offer from my sister's husband to work for/with him in a new and potentially very lucrative venture that he began after having worked for NY Telephone. I said yes, resigned from Heath and flew back home to NYC.

My Ricky Nelson "Travelin' Man" days were over.

17
YOU CANNOT GO HOME AGAIN

So, there I was. A 25-year-old champion of his world moving back home with the parents. Not since the tender age of 17 (was it really eight years?) did I live in that Brooklyn apartment, and it did not take long to come to the realization that my sanity was at risk if I stayed much longer. My parents did nothing wrong mind you, but for anyone and everyone that has been there done that, I do not think any further explanation is necessary.

New York City is an exceptionally large piece of American terrain. I knew most of Brooklyn and parts of other boroughs from childhood adventures but as an adult, New York City had one identifier –the island of Manhattan.

I dare say the Dutch had not a clue what they were buying for the equivalent of $24. Without a doubt, Manhattan is the most diverse and exciting piece of real estate on the planet. Not so much, however, when looking for a place to live. Rents, even back then, were extremely high and competition from a zillion baby-boomers to find suitable lodging was off the charts. Going it alone without a roommate just made it a little harder to find an affordable place. I did!

The Upper -East side area of Manhattan is an above average income neighborhood. Real estate studies reveal that this neighborhood has a higher income than 76% of the neighborhoods in America, except where I found a place.

The south side of E. 92nd Street and 1st Avenue (not to be confused with E.92nd Street in Brooklyn) geographically defines the northern limit of the Upper East Side. To the north is Spanish Harlem. Does West Side Story or Ben E. King's There is a Red Rose Up in Spanish Harlem ring a bell? On the south side one can find a grocery store. On the north side, it is a bodega (a Hispanic/Spanish/Latin mini-mart, kind of like a 7-11, but usually smaller and more of a liquor store atmosphere. The word came from the actual Spanish word for "grocery store" - la bodega).

I moved into a third-floor walk-up studio and was paying $165/month in rent. For this arrangement I had one small room with an open kitchen, one closet and a small bathroom with a shower and a vertical steam pipe that was the devil incarnate. Yes, it provided nice steam heat but maneuvering around it to shower was akin to playing Russian roulette. I still have the burn scars on my back!

I did not have any roommates, at least not of the humankind. Cockroaches will be on this planet for eternity. They cannot be eliminated, only coaxed to move next door. I was "lucky" to have them as permanent houseguests as well as those from my neighbors. With the lights off, all was usually OK other than for the occasional one or two that used me as a shortcut to move across the room. In the morning and/or with the lights turned on, I had an audience. My furnishings at first included a folding cot with a mattress, an old dresser, and a small round kitchen table with two chairs, all donated to me by caring relatives. Come to think of it, my upgrades were non-existent. I endured shouting matches in Spanish between my neighbors, the sounds and smells of unimaginable origin and occasional firecrackers (or was it gunshots?) on the streets. To me, however, it was the Taj Mahal! Home!

I was collaborating with my new brother-in-law and his business partners in an office on Union Square in lower Manhattan. I was a whiz at mastering the IRT Lexington #6 express from E. 86th to E. 14th Street daily. Only on a NYC subway can one get to see shows that cannot be beat. Off-key saxophone players; want to-be Broadway singers; pick pockets, drunks, junkies in a stupor and all for the price of a subway token. In fact, another one of the funniest things I ever saw was with an attractive African American female holding onto the center support pole in the subway car for balance. A short, wiry sort of kid also grabbed that pole and began undulating to the rhythm of the train in an obvious and provocative manner in the direction of the woman. Now realize that when that express train is racing at breakneck speed, the decibel level inside the train is as loud as a jet engine and it is difficult to be heard without shouting. This woman disproved that assumption when she simply turned her face toward that young man and in a whisper-quiet tone that many nearby heard loud and clear said "don't you ride ME, Jack, you ride this train." He melted into the crowd and life resumed with civility. Bully for her! For all I know she may as well have gone into politics.

18
So Much Fun – So Little Time

My late twenties were a blur. Suffice it to say there were many good times. After about a year of poverty on E. 92nd Street I made it to the big time – East 85th Street & 1st Ave. My rent had gone up to $225/month and the amount of space was not much more. And yes, again I had the non-human species keep me company. It was a great neighborhood. The bars were everywhere. So was marijuana. Back then that stuff was everywhere, inexpensive (and illegal) and although usually mildly potent, it was no match to what is on the streets today.

Manhattan is a fabulous place to meet people for any number of reasons, friendships being among them. I used to "hang out" at a bar called the Hazard Powder Company. My peers and I would grab floor space, guzzle a beer or two, listen to music and wind down the day. I struck up a friendship with another Steve and we got along famously. We were both rock 'n roll fans – he loved Mott the Hoople and Jethro Tull whereas I was a diehard Stones fan. We attended live concerts at Madison Square Garden including The Who (Queen was the opening act), Iron Butterfly and many others.

Steve's parents owned a retail fish store on 1st Ave and E. 73rd Street as well as the railroad flat above the store where Steve lived. A railroad flat is an apartment of contiguous rooms all in a row from front to back. He also had the best grass and hash! We would take and unwind to great music and on occasion we would share that experience with other friends we met (yes, females just to be clear).

His apartment reeked from the illicit substances, which I suppose added to the entire experience. The trouble was that the apartment was only accessed by climbing up a long and narrow wooden staircase that was not what one would consider an engineering marvel. Going up was easy despite the alcohol in my system. It was the prospect of negotiating going back down at 1:00 am after getting stoned. One look down and I opted for the extremely comfortable couch. Leaving to walk back home at 7:00 am to clean up for work was much easier. It became a routine. We lost touch years later, but the great memories remain.

19
MAKING A LIFE

I viewed the opportunity of collaborating with my brother-in-law as the lesser of two options. One was a paycheck; the other was no paycheck. Now in all fairness, he did offer me a unique approach at making money based on personal effort. There was a salary a little better than what I was making at Heath, with a steady paycheck in hand weekly and the potential to earn much more money via commissions from the sharing in the refunds we would obtain for customers of NY Telephone.

The deal was simple. Visit customers that return a prepaid postcard expressing an interest to save money. NY Telephone was, as he learned from working there, notoriously but erroneously overbilling many of its customers for the equipment that they rented each month. This had nothing to do with calls. Long before the breakup of the AT&T monopoly and before the advent of non-telephone company equipment every customer paid Ma Bell for everything from the land lines, tie lines, switchboards, telephone desk sets, ringers, relays, lights and so much more. Installers made errors and the bills generated from such installations often included equipment that was possibly either never requested, miscoded and/or incorrectly listed on the records. A simple billing error such as for a handset that was never installed could, over a few years, add up to a lot of money and have been paid unknowingly out of the customer's pocket. More significant errors such as for never installed lines or more sophisticated equipment yielded a treasure trove to be tapped for the customer's benefit.

I would visit potential customers to "sign them up" by obtaining their written authorization to obtain their equipment charge records from NY Telephone on their behalf. The potential customer had absolutely nothing to lose. If we found errors in their favor, we would obtain a refund for them going back as far as possible. The deal was that we would split the refund 50/50 with the customer who would then also have a corrected (and lower) bill going forward. Most customers saw this as a win-win and eagerly signed up. Others were a bit skeptical and needed a nudge. That was easy. I would place two $10 bills on their desk and ask if it would be OK if I did this every month and just took one back as I left. Deal!

It is funny but the tougher corporate customers that had a communications manager were the hardest to convince. That was because those managers feared they would be seen as incompetent if we were able to do what they could not do on their own. What a novel idea? My brother-in-law worked extremely hard and deserved a richly rewarding lifestyle as a result. Unfortunately, the fit for me was just not there so I left the position in late 1974 and moved on.

My single life in Manhattan rolled along fine! I had saved a little money, and with the aid of MasterCard debt, I was the champion of my universe.

So, what now? What did I want to do for a living? Driving a cab was too scary a thought. So, I figured now would be a suitable time to complete the needed classes to earn my college degree. With consent from the NCSU registrar, I enrolled in two math classes at Hunter College (part of the City College of NY) located a short distance from my apartment. I did not understand the purpose, use or value of either class but they were less difficult that I expected, and I passed both easily.

A few weeks later there was a cardboard tube in my mailbox. I retrieved it, opened it, and marveled at my Bachelor of Science degree diploma. My wake-up call arrived.

20
SUN FUN

In the 1970s, the NYC's "in-place" during the summers was a beach house someplace along the Long Island south shore. Thousands of baby boomers followed like lemmings to Fire Island, NY, an overgrown sandbar of an island accessible via the Long Island Railroad to Patchogue, NY then via a ferry to various towns across Long Island Sound.

Beach communities there had numerous summer rental properties and those young urbanites with means rented 4, 5- or 6-bedroom houses for the summer and sublet rooms each weekend. It was common for a 4-bedroom house to have two bunk beds per room - or twelve people per weekend. For a ridiculously low price per weekend "A" and "B" shares of alternating weekends or about eight weekends per share, were rented. Midweek stays were at no extra cost other than one's own provisions.

Finding out about the shares was easy. For many years, the underground alternative to the mainstream NY dailies, The Village Voice newspaper (ceased publication in 2017 but made a digital comeback in 2021), had listings in the classified section. Manhattan house parties were the meeting places where the lessor(s) met the potential renters. This informal selection process as to who might be lucky enough to get a sublet share was akin to the pledge party scene in Animal House. No ugly-looking, nerdy or overly obese kids ever made the cut. Hey, it was the 70's, remember?

My first summer-share was in the summer of 1972 after I returned to Brooklyn following the job with Heath and beginning work with my brother-in-law. The beach house was leased by a guy named "Buddy" (remember this name for later) who then sublet the weekend shares as described above.

Buddy was an attorney of modest means but short on business savvy. He neglected, or declined to, seek damage deposit escrows from the weekenders. Among the benefits of unwinding in a summer beach house, aside from top notch doobies, Sangria, and unabashed sex, was tasty food!

I bet I've got your attention now!

One person on the weekend roster oversaw placing the grocery order at the store in Patchogue. Food orders were paid in cash on account and boxes of the food with names were placed on a special food ferry to the stipulated landing dock (ours was Davis Park). The honor system worked great! The food was then picked up by housemates dragging a little red wagon across boardwalks over the sand. It was an almost flawless process. Friday night was arrival time for the housemates and there was no dinner schedule. Burgers and hot dogs were available for grilling along with side snacks, beer, and wine. Saturday night: however, was more ritualistic and those self-proclaimed and pre-identified weekend cooks prepared dinner for everyone. A vision of the biblical Last Supper table comes to mind.

Anyway, one Saturday evening the cooks prepared an impressive roast in the house's oven. As the rack holding the roasting pan was slid forward, it clattered and fell onto the

Linoleum-tiled kitchen floor. The roast was spared disaster via the helping hands, but one housemate suffered a hand burn (not too serious) as the oven rack fell and the floor was scorched.

The owner of the home was upset to hear of this incident and fully expected Buddy, per their contractual agreement, to pay for the damage repair. Buddy balked and claimed negligence on the cooks who told Buddy to, well, you know. Buddy the lawyer opted for a strategy to collect and subpoena everyone that was there that weekend to appear in small claims court in lower Manhattan. We all had to go and so, we did.

Small Claims Court officials are called Magistrates. They are civil court officers or lay judges that administer the law that deals with minor offenses. Our Magistrate was an older Jewish man (he looked to be in his eighties to us). He sat at the head of a large conference table, we mostly sat around the table and the others just stood. Buddy presented his case. The Magistrate then began a slow comprehension of what this house looked like and asked,

"How many bedrooms?"

"4"

"How many people?"

"12"

"Boys & Girls?"

"Yes"

"Separate accommodations for boys and girls?"

"Not always."

"How many bathrooms?"

"2"

The Magistrate looked up, expressionless, cleared his throat, and continued by asking each housemate individually what each was doing at the time of this incident. Answers included playing my guitar, sitting on the deck, making the salad, taking a shower, etc. The Magistrate then asked if Buddy was an attorney, Buddy replied "Yes, your honor, I am."

The Magistrate tersely replied: "Sonny, didn't they teach you in law school to never represent yourself?" He added, "Next time, don't be such a schmuck." The case was dismissed. Buddy paid the damages and we all then, out of pity, took Buddy out for Chinese food.

For the summer of 1973, I repeated this summer tradition, but with a bit of a wrinkle. I had been dating a girl in Manhattan for several months and we both wanted to get summer shares; however, there was some friction in our relationship, and we decided it would be best if we stayed in different houses. The friction stemmed from her desire to experiment with more than just grass and hash. Not my style as I was afraid of stuff like Quaaludes, LSD, and cocaine. Long story short, the guys that rented the house had two houses and an error was made in the housing assignments. Not only did we end up in the same house, but we were also assigned the outside screened-in-room (it had rain shutters).

Well, we were a "couple," so it was easy to see why or how we ended up in the same room. There were three beds. We had pushed two together (oh do not act so surprised) and the third bed was vacant – for a while!

21
JAW DROP TIME

Midway through this summer, the third bed was assigned to a lovely, attractive young woman who had sought the "peace and quiet" of a summer share. Does the term awkward come to mind? I will leave the details out, but I am sure there was quite a bit of embarrassment with this arrangement. This new young lady remained in the house long enough to realize that this experience was not what she had in mind.

I liked her, and I suppose "hit on her" at the house parties but she did not appear interested. I could hardly blame her. My (now ex) girlfriend and I ended our relationship that summer when she moved in with a guy with similar indulgent desires to experiment with psychotic drugs.

In mid-1973 I took a trip to Club Med on the French island of Martinique in the Caribbean with two friends. During this trip I knew I had to become organized when I get back to New York and get a real job. I had not yet found employment - or true love but I did have to continue my quest for both. On October 6, 1974, a little over a year after the last Fire Island summer house I was back on E. 85th Street and I received a phone call.

In case you have not figured it out, Linda was the nice young lady that shared that room in the summer house. The lease to Linda's studio apartment on E. 82nd Street at 1st Avenue was expiring and she was out looking for new digs with assistance from a realtor. They happened to stop at my building to check on a vacancy when she remembered from our rides home from the beach that I lived here. While inside the building with the realtor she decided to leave a note under my door as I was not home at the time. The problem was that I lived in apartment 1E on the second floor, and she mistakenly left the note under the door of apartment L (lobby) E.

She then went home and waited for my call that never came. So, determined to find me, she called 411 information and obtained my listed phone number. She called later and when I answered she asked if I knew who this is. I did! She then asked if I got her note.

Note? What note? I said hold on and raced down to LE, that vacant apartment, and luckily was able to open the door and retrieve her note. We chatted and agreed to meet at Carl Schurz Park the next day where I was doing a photo shoot (photography was a hobby of mine) for Our Town, the local upper eastside neighborhood newspaper.

So, at about 2:00 pm on a beautiful NYC fall afternoon we met at the park. She was a vision decked out in a boat-neck top and jeans. Her hair was all in place, and she had on makeup and perfume. Of course, I had no idea how long she primped for this meeting. I, on the other hand was a sweaty mess wearing a t-shirt and had a camera and lenses hanging around my neck. With more work to do I suggested she meet me for dinner at my apartment. She agreed.

I hit the grocery for what to prepare (Cornish hens, a salad, and a nice bottle of wine), got home, and cleaned up. The cooking was a disaster. I overcooked (burned) the hens and smoke billowed out of the oven. My apartment was now a cloud. She stepped into the hall for some fresher air and met my neighbor Dennis.

Linda and Dennis struck up a conversation that continued down the hall in HIS apartment. I recalled Dennis was in psychological therapy like 4 days a week and realized that this was not a good situation, so I "rescued" her, and we did our best at dining on what was left of the hens.

We began dating and after several weeks of our relationship, she told me that her property owner needed to paint her apartment and she asked if she could stay with me for a few days. So suddenly there we were she, me and her non-housebroken Yorkie, Leopold, living in my cramped studio.

I someow sensed that my life was changing. It did. I did not have any idea at the time that she eventually would be my forever soulmate. She claims that she knew this immediately – or so she has told me so repeatedly. It has now been over 46 years since she moved into my life. Thank heaven, she never moved out!

22
IN LOVING MEMORY

In 1960, at age 13 my "Bar-Mitzvah" was held in Brooklyn's Kings Highway Jewish Center with the reception following at the Elite Club which was close to where mom, Julie, and I lived. Nana was in failing health with heart problems and passed away soon after. She was indeed special to me, and Gramps would tell me over and over after she passed away how thankful she was to witness my right of passage.

Gramps grieved but eventually took on the persona of a wealthy widower and toured the world on cruise ships. Think "Where's Waldo?" and my cousins and I would laugh at the post cards and soon we were amused at his array of "lady-friends." As with Nana, he too succumbed from heart trouble (attributed to heavy smoking) and passed away at age 83 while I was frolicking on that Fire Island beach when I was twenty-seven. I will never forget the bittersweet moment of both excitement and sorrow. I miss my grandpa and nana dearly. Nana Becky was also present to witness my Bar Mitzvah (Grampa Max had passed several years prior).

23
EPIPHANY

Relationships are all about sharing. As youngsters we learn to share toys and/or clothes, though generally not without squabbles. When we mature, we become more independent and turn away from criticism. As stated earlier I was not a great student. Teachers and well-meaning family members cajoled me repeatedly that I was not applying myself and that I was much brighter and smarter that what my grades showed because of my lack of effort. How does one react to such comments? In short, one ignores them and keeps moving in the hopes that some miraculous change will happen.

So, there I was, still no real job and still with a lack of motivation. I did, however, have an apartment and a beautiful girlfriend. The apartment was simply rented real estate. The girlfriend was everything else and through her belief in me, the seeds of motivation were planted.

Wanting something to raise my self-esteem and my economic standing (not mutually exclusive ideals) moved me to take the reins so I met with an occupational counselor. For a small fee I was evaluated for aptitude, skill sets, a history of my education and employment, personality, and interests as necessary to ensure the best possible result. Much was revealed through the thorough interviewing process after the testing. The information was then applied to job fields I might want to consider.

My counselor carefully reviewed everything and knew I had a penchant and an aptitude for technical work. He suggested I consider talking and working with an insurance carrier about conducting fire protection inspections and the fact that my work at Heath often included crawling within buildings might be a positive advantage. What did I have to lose?

So, I got back to the apartment and opened the Manhattan telephone directory to the section on insurance carriers. Starting with the A's, I made it down to American International Group (AIG). I spoke with the personnel department (I do not think HR was the invented term yet) and was invited to interview with the Loss Control Manager. Whoa!

I took the subway down to the Wall Street area and found my way to 70 Pine Street. I met with the AIG Loss Control Manager who explained to me what the job was about. He handed me a recently written Builder's Risk Loss Control Report to underwriting concerning the construction of a new E.J. Korvette's department store in Brooklyn that was built partially over a marina, and he asked that I look it over and see if I had any questions. I did. I mentioned that I did not see any commentary as to the use of pressurized lumber in areas over or near the water. The lack of such would certainly lead to wood rot and serious property damage. He took the report back, glanced at it and without expression, put it on a pile and asked me if I would like a job. I accepted the offer and was told to report for classroom training that would last about two weeks followed by field training.

I learned a lot about fire protection engineering principles, calculated the effectiveness of water supplies, tested fire pumps, etc. It was all new and exciting,

Thus, in April 1975 my new career was born. Further, now I had my college degree, a delightful place to live, and a girlfriend that genuinely cared about me. She was proud of me…and so was I!

Linda worked as a secretary to James (Jim) Lipton (yes, the same James Lipton of the Actor's Studio TV show years later). Linda assisted Jim with scripts for the Guiding Light TV soap opera, taped daily in NYC. My name (and status) was elevated via being cast on one show as Dr. Damsker and my assistant was Nurse Lieberman (all thanks to Linda's script editing and Jim's OK). For harmony, one episode also featured our Yorkie as Dr. Leopold.

Jim was also influential in NYC's entertainment elite. That translated into getting tickets to sold-out shows. He graciously surprised us via his Madison Square Garden contacts with near front row seats to the Rolling Stone sold out "Tour of the Americas '75."

This was the Rolling Stones' first tour with new guitarist Ronnie Wood and Billy Preston on keyboards. At the start of the concert the stage was in the shape of a folded Lotus leaf. The lights went out and the spotlight hit the stage just as the Lotus leaf petals began unfolding to the opening guitar riff for "Honky-Tonk Women." The Garden atmosphere was electric (and pungent)! I had my trusted Minolta 101 35mm SLR at the ready and took impressive black & white photos that I self-developed and printed and I still have them. Way cool!

24
MIXED BLESSINGS

Linda & I pooled our resources and we upgraded by moving into a one-bedroom apartment on the 10th floor at 233 E. 69th Street. There was even a door attendant. We made the big time for about $400/month. Our friend Bruce from Fire Island days had a truck associated with his coffee shop business and helped with the move.

Although it seemed like only a mile or so, we made it with a minimum of furniture breakage while weaving in general, stopping for lights, and hitting a few potholes. With the aid (ahem, tipping) of some young building workers, we were moved in!

Political learning experiences are best homed in NYC. One is never too far from an opportunity to gain from the barter system – the lifeblood of the city. The superintendent (most buildings had one) was Carmine. He spoke with a thick Italian accent and was not too good with English. We chatted one day about some repairs that I needed done and then I mentioned I had to go upstairs as Linda was cooking stuffed cabbage for dinner. His eyes widened right away. I knew. So, after dinner I knocked on his basement apartment door and presented him and his wife with a pot of the stuffed cabbage (Linda never did pay attention to portion control). He was thrilled. A few days later I had a reciprocal knock on our door and was presented with a tureen of the best smelling and tasting Italian sausage and meatballs. Delicious! To parody the quote from Humphrey Bogart to Claude Rains at the end of the 1942 film Casablanca, "Carmine, I think this could be the beginning of a beautiful friendship". Indeed, it was.

I have always been a believer that things in life happen for a reason. Sometimes the reason is obvious, but sometimes it is disguised. At some point earlier in 1975 I worked up the courage to ask Linda to marry me. She knew this would be a fait accompli (an accomplished fact; a thing already done) long before I asked and so the deal was sealed with an opal ring and a kiss. We, then, with her parent's blessing, decided we would get married in May of 1976. Planning was underway.

At AIG, the one thing I could NOT do well was engineering drawings (diagrams). Close up detail was not in my genetic code and my inability to do this led to my dismissal about a year later. It was April 1976 to be more precise.

Being laid off (a not-so-nice term for being fired) was traumatic but for whatever reason I was not worried. I met with a recruiter that specializes in insurance work and was presented with an opportunity to interview with M&M Protection Consultants (M&MPC), the Loss Control department of the prestigious insurance brokerage firm of Marsh & McLennan. I did so and was told I would hear from them regarding a decision shortly. On May 29, 1976, the evening prior to our wedding, I received a call from the assistant manager. He knew about the wedding plans and told me he was giving us a wedding present as the job was mine when I returned from the honeymoon to Bermuda – and oh yes, the pay was 33% higher than what I was earning at AIG!

Linda & I were married May 30, 1976, at the International Synagogue at JFK International Airport and had the party at Feathers in the Park at Flushing Meadows NY on the site of the 1964 World's fair, and in the shadow of Shea Stadium, home of the NY Mets. We spent the night at a hotel near JFK and then flew out on Eastern Airlines to Bermuda for our honeymoon.

M&MPC knew I had limited experience but saw it as an opportunity to pay me less than a more senior employee and in turn they could bill clients at a slightly lower rate. I was assigned to teams collaborating with corporate giants including WR Grace, Seagram, and AT&T. I served as an intermediary with the insurance carrier loss control departments, conducted reviews of survey reports and offered additional recommendations as needed. I learned a lot quickly. In 1977, M&MPC moved our department offices from midtown Manhattan to Morristown NJ. That was our ticket out of the Big Apple. It was time.

We found a nice 1-bedroom garden apartment in Budd Lake NJ, and we made friends with many other young couples. Ironically, at a party at one of our neighbors, I noted a photo album on their cocktail table. The man in the photo looked remarkably familiar to me. The party host, Eddie, confirmed my suspicion. It was his brother-in-law, Buddy. Remember Buddy? I told Eddie about Fire Island and the subpoenas, and he then validated that Magistrate's comment by saying "Buddy is such a schmuck."

Not too long after we moved into the Budd Lake apartment, sadness struck when Julie passed away following a lengthy battle with lung cancer. He was sixty-seven. My memory of him and our life together remains with me. I still find myself thinking of the guidance or advice he would offer. My one regret was that his laughter and kindness could never be shared with my children to be.

After a year and a half of renting we moved to Hopatcong NJ and purchased a bi-level money pit. By July 1979, I was employed with M&MPC for about 4-years and was no longer "feeling the love." I was a member of the NYC chapter of the Society of Fire Protection Engineers (SFPE), and I had good networking contacts which resulted in a call to me from a manager at a competing insurance brokerage company, Johnson & Higgins (J&H). The Senior Manager heard via the grapevine that I was unhappy at M&MPC and wanted to talk with me about an opportunity. I was surprised that he knew about me. He was interested in hiring me except for the fact that unlike with M&MPC, J&H only wanted to hire those that had a PE (Professional Engineer) designation. He; however, had a better idea and came back at me with an option. One of their corporate clients, City Investing Company, was looking for a Loss Control Manager and he wanted to recommend me to them for the job. If I got the job, it would also help further their continuing relationship with City Investing.

For several months, nine to be more precise, Linda was working on an incredibly special "project" which was completed at 8:41 AM on September 15, 1980, at Morristown Memorial Hospital. Melanie Joy Damsker, weighing in at 8lbs, 3 oz. greeted her new parents. To say the least, I was excited on so many levels. Mom, baby, and I were all doing well.

25
JOB PROGRESSION

In the world of risk control, I found the "pecking" order to first have a job with the insurance carrier, then an upgrade to the insurance broker, and then onto a management position with an industrial corporation. Hence the opportunity to speak with the Risk Manager at City Investing Company was welcomed. City Investing was a conglomerate headquartered in Beverly Hills, CA. Manufacturing subsidiaries included Rheem Mfg. (water heaters and air conditioning), Guerdon Inc. (mobile home mfg.) World Color Press Inc., (magazine publishing and printing) UARCO Inc. (business forms printing), Hayes International Corp (military and commercial aircraft modifications and repairs), and others. A non-manufacturing subsidiary included the Home Insurance Company. My interview was scheduled with Dan McCarthy, City Investing's Risk Manager. We met at Rheem's NYC office on Park Avenue. When I arrived for the interview, I was in shock to see a few AIG former coworkers also there for the job. I did not think I had a chance. Dan and I talked a bit, and I did my best to answer his questions. He told me I would be contacted one way or the other within a few days.

About 2 weeks went by and not hearing from Dan I called his office in CA to inquire. His Executive Assistant, Rachel, told me that Dan suffered an appendicitis attack, had surgery and was recovering at home BUT she said Dan would like to talk with me again. For fun (and Brownie points) I sent him a get-well card with a note that I did not think our meeting would have such a drastic effect on his health. Within a few days, his HR Manager (that term finally arrived to replace Personnel) called and asked if I could fly to LA to talk more with Dan (at their expense of course). I did in late August 1980 and was greeted at LAX by the J&H property insurance brokerage West Coast Team.

We drove to Dan's house in Woodland Hills, in the San Fernando Valley. The casualty brokerage team, Frank B. Hall Inc., was also in attendance and as we all sat around his pool to discuss next year's insurance renewals Dan mentioned the tasks that I would need to perform in this process. Gulp! Suddenly he paused and with a grin in front of everyone he looked at me and asked if I will be joining the company. The joke was on me. They all knew long before I got there that they wanted ME! I nodded yes without so much as a thought to the contrary. After the meeting I met with the J&H contact who told me they knew more about me than I knew. They vetted me, liked my background, personality, and gumption. How could I refuse? I did, however, have one small "worry."

My background was in fire protection and the job as Loss Control Manager also included safety as in OSHA compliance, surveys, and training. So, prior to leaving LA I called Dan and expressed appreciation for his hiring me but needed him to know that safety management was not my specialty. He laughed, repeated how I was vetted and said property is the hard part. You know what to do there. With safety, you can learn as you go. We know who we hired and that is all you need to know, plus the broker's loss control people will assist so do not worry, you will be just fine. That worked for me. I called Linda and told her I accepted the City Investing job with a starting date in October, on Rheem's payroll and would have an office in NYC. I then flew back to NJ and shortly after I resigned from M&MPC.

26
CALIFORNIA DREAMING

Between October and December, I was flying all the time to subsidiary facilities. I was also asked to attend a meeting in LA so Melanie's Nana Diane watched her for a few days while nervous Linda and I spent a few days in CA. New wrinkle time! Dan told me that he planned to retire, and that City Investing will be moving all its CA operations to NYC. He said that most of the staff knew this and hence left earlier for other jobs, which is why there is so much dependence on the insurance brokers, but he needed me to be the company's face to direct the day-to-day risk control function and serve as the insurance liaison. Further, it would be best for me and for the company if I worked out of California for the next six months.

Would I come out with Linda and the baby, and they would pay for a condominium rental and a car lease for the six-month period. Now let us think about this…spend 6 months in freezing snowy New Jersey with long daily bus commutes or live in LA with balmy weather and an easy commute with a leased car?

We closed the New Jersey house, shipped out our car for Linda's use and we moved to West LA (close to Santa Monica) on Feb. 1, 1980. Life was good. We were a short drive west to the Santa Monica beach and a short drive east to City Investing's Beverly Hills office building. Some tenants in this building also included attorneys to Hollywood movie and TV stars. It was common to see famous people in the elevators. On occasion Linda would bring Melanie for a lunch date with me and she met some of the stars. At other times Linda would stroll along the Santa Monica beach area with Melanie and collect autographs from the stars who all naturally fawned over Melanie! Who could blame them!?

27
MR. NICE GUY IS AN OXYMORON

As stated, although I worked for City Investing, I was on the Rheem payroll and my position reported locally to Rheem's President. With the move back east and my new office in the Park Avenue building, Rheem's President stopped into my office soon after I began working there and said that he would like me to visit all of Rheem's manufacturing facilities within a year. This of course, was in addition to my need to visit many other City Investing locations. So, I once again was a road warrior but now with an American Express card! My responsibilities increased and I was busier than I could have imagined but it was all working out great.

Rheem's operations were all over the US and in Puerto Rico. I asked if he wanted me to visit down there as well. He said, "whenever you are ready." Soon thereafter, I came home and handed Linda an envelope with two airline tickets from Newark to San Juan with accommodations at the Caribe Hilton for a few days. Nana Diane was again summoned to watch Melanie.

The job was great. I loved it. I felt comfortable and was a respected presence whenever I visited any of the City's facilities – with exceptions. The role of a corporate Risk Control Manager is to evaluate potential losses and recommend actions to take to reduce or eliminate such loss threats. It is a technique that utilizes findings from risk assessments, which involve identifying potential risk factors in a company's operations, such as technical and non-technical aspects of the business, financial policies and other issues that may affect the well-being of the firm. Risk control also helps companies limit lost assets and income.

Some facility management personnel were not, shall I say, open and honest and at times would hide known problems rather than deal with them, especially if doing so impacted their profits. It was rare that I would not discover such non-compliance items. When I did, relationships caused friction. A lot of it.

28
REALITY WAKE-UP CALL

I visited Air International Inc. at the Clearwater/St. Pete, FL airport. Air International was also part of Hayes International with facilities at the Birmingham, AL airport. Both Air International and Hayes International were aircraft maintenance and repair facilities. Air International worked on domestic air carriers such as Newark NJ-based Peoples Express, and Hayes was a military contractor that worked on USAF aircraft. Following a tour of the Air International facility I pointed out to the manager some environmental regulatory infractions that needed to be addressed. In this case, aircraft washing was performed on the tarmac but the pumps to move the contaminated water from the drains to a containment area for treatment were not working.

Furthermore, the wastewater treatment containment area had holes in the walls and could not contain any spillage from storage/treatment tanks. I explained the concern as a financial and a legal issue and that if these issues were not addressed, regulatory laws would be impacted, and substantial fines might result. I was told they would address these issues.

A few days later, a US Coast Guard aircraft (the USCG base was adjacent to the Clearwater airport) was flying over the Air International facility on a landing approach to the USCG base following a heavy rainstorm and noted a plume of water pollution flowing from our operations into

Tampa Bay. The USCG called the Florida EPA and then the Florida EPA called the Air International Manager that I had previously met. The Air International Manager then had to call his boss in Birmingham to advise him of the call from the Florida EPA, who would be visiting the Air International operations the next day. That evening I received a call at home in NJ from the President of Hayes Int'l in Birmingham AL requesting me to fly down from Newark Int'l. to Tampa/Clearwater the next morning, for the meeting. I did so and I managed to mitigate some issues as to the actual chemical pollutants and thus effected some financial damage control at the meeting with the Florida EPA, but there still would be cleanup costs and a hefty fine.

The Air International facility manager was angry with me (heck all I did was point this out to him earlier) because Corporate was now involved. He told me he had a good mind to fly to NYC and tell my boss what he thought about me and the way I conducted my job. I handed him my AMEX card and being somewhat of a smart ass myself said "Here… go first class on me." He declined and offered me a few choice words instead. Corporate life can be harsh.

29
AND THE HITS KEEP COMING

The Occupational Safety & Health Administration is one of the most powerful Federal agencies and violating workplace safety laws often result in expensive fines. Compliance was often a challenge, and I was the one that assisted the plants with training and compliance. It was not easy, but I was proud of, and earned a lot of respect for what I did.

My job spanned a wide scope of loss potentials including environmental, property and safety. The mix was never dull. The USEPA is another powerful agency. Knowing what I had discovered in FL, I was requested by the Hayes Birmingham management to conduct a little due diligence there as well. Oh boy!

In 1980 a new environmental law regulating hazardous wastes was created by Congress called the Resource Conservation & Recovery Act (RCRA). I noted some anomalies in the way hazardous wastes were handled by Hayes personnel, but I was advised that they had secured an agreement with a recycler to remove spent solvent wastes for treatment and resale of the cleaned liquids and that this recycler would transport the solid wastes to the secured landfills for legal disposal at no extra cost if they had the recycle agreement.

This seemed OK until drums of solid wastes ended up in public dumps and/or areas where they should never have been placed. Hayes and the parent City Investing Company were indicted by the Federal government for reckless endangerment. A $250K fine was assessed and a Hayes facilities operator was sentenced to in jail for gross negligence associated with violations of the RCRA act. Not so fast! I reviewed the regulations carefully and then conferred with attorneys.

It was a long shot, but I discovered a loophole regarding the actual definition and identification of the term hazardous waste mixtures. An appeal was pursued based on my findings, and the convictions were reversed by the appellate court that had assessed the recycler, which filed for bankruptcy and went out of business, a $25,000 fine - and the Hayes fine was reduced to $25,000 and all other charges, including the jail sentence were dismissed.

30
SEPARATION ANXIETY OR WHAT COMES AROUND GOES AROUND

Just prior to the closing of the Beverly Hills office in June of 1981, I attended a meeting in California with the Home Insurance's senior people from NYC along with City Investing Company's replacement for my retired boss, Dan. A new Risk Manager was recently hired from another industrial corporation and attended the meeting in California. My family and I were about to be relocated back to New Jersey J and move back into our Lake Hopatcong money pit.

While it began as a friendly meeting it quickly changed when I vented my frustrations as to how the home was price gouging the insurance premiums of the sister companies as the "in house" insurance carrier, not allowing competitive bids, and in many cases not willing to settle worker's comp claims "fairly." I figured after I got back to NYC, I would have to find another job. The distrust was mutual.

When the return to NYC was completed, my new boss asked me to meet him for dinner. I was fully expecting a termination. On the contrary, he told me that the Home wanted me out for not being a "team player" but he knew the job I did, and he needed me. He told me that he told them NO WAY and since he was "higher" than the Home's brass, I was staying, and I remained on the Home payroll. The Home was not happy.

Linda & I decided it was time to sell the house and move closer to NYC for an easier commute. We rented a 2-bedroom condominium in Old Bridge, NJ. My travels with City continued and I visited operations from New York to Florida to California and many locations in between.

Linda remained a stay-at-home mom in New Jersey. In December 1982 I attended a meeting in California with the brokers. I called home to check on things and Linda confirmed that we were now expecting child number two!!! BIG yay! On Sept. 26, 1983, 8lb. 13oz Amy Lynne greeted the world. Now we had to find more space! Luckily, there was a larger unit for sale in the neighborhood, so we stopped being renters, bought it, and moved in.

31
Breaking Up is (Not Always) Hard to Do

By 1984, I had been with City Investing for four years, first on Rheem's payroll, then on the Home Insurance payroll. City Investing was now going through with a leveraged buyout (LBO) through Kolberg, Kravits

Roberts (KKR) for the purpose of breaking it up and selling the parts. A leveraged buyout is a popular financial action but very unpopular with employees that would be laid off after years of service. I was reassured that my department would be part of the buyout and transferred to a new holding company named Pace Industries. The deal was such that all of City's manufacturing subsidiaries would be sold and be retained by Pace and that the non-manufacturing companies including the Home Insurance Company would not be part of the deal. The Home was elated to rid themselves of the City's Risk Management department and I along with my three co-workers were given termination notices effective at the close of business on 12/31/84, and that we would be given severance pay. Home was livid to learn that on 01/2/85 we were working in the same capacity in the same building, on a different floor, but now for Pace. We kept the severance checks! About a week later, the Home's Chief Financial Officer came up to our office demanding we turn over all the loss control files. I declined. He asked if I knew who he is.

I said I know who you were. He left empty handed. If ever there was a middle finger moment for me, that was it.

32
CHANGING DIAPERS AND CHANGING STRIPES

Late in 1987 the hammer began to fall as it was announced that some of Pace's companies would be broken up and sold as was the case with City Investing but I did not think my job was as secure and rather than risk a layoff notice, I opted to look elsewhere. By this time, I had not only honed my prowess in property and environmental issues but was now adept at safety and worker's compensation matters. Via my membership and participation in the NYC chapter of American Society of Safety Engineers, a business acquaintance mentioned to me that he was vacating his position in NYC with Westvaco Corporation – a paper manufacturing company with subsidiary operations. He knew of my situation and asked me to speak with his manager, Rudy, about replacing his position with me.

Rudy and I met and talked, and Rudy asked that I speak with Manny, the engineering manager who was a stern, elderly Jewish man with a Napoleonic complex. Manny and I then chatted a while and I dropped a few Yiddish comments for good measure. Manny began to smile and said, "I am not allowed to ask, but are you Jewish?" I nodded yes. He said this is a very "Waspy" company with very few Jews. I said, "Well this will make two of us." I also mentioned to him I had a cousin that used to sell corrugated board products. He asked who and when I told him he lit up. The cousin was my late great Uncle Milton (Cousin George's father). Manny said he was a clerk for Milton in the 1940s. I told him I had a VHS tape from old home movies if he wanted to see it. He did. He told Rudy to hire me.

On 10/1/87 I relocated to another office on Park Avenue as the Safety Manager for the 12-plant corrugated container division. The next day I showed Manny the tape. We were best buds now – until we went to Richmond.

Manny oversaw the expansion and the construction changes to a Westvaco flexographic printing plant. This also included the upgrade and expansion of the plant's heating, air conditioning and ventilation system (HVAC) and he asked me to travel down there with him to indoctrinate me. He was old school and as such we traveled by train! The first thing I saw was the large new expanded duct work which was now completely blocking the ceiling-level automatic fire suppression automatic sprinkler system heads. I pointed this out and Manny said, "So what?" "We have never had a fire and we won't and besides, it would cost too much to re-engineer everything."

I could NOT let this happen. On a break I called Rudy who was furious that Manny would do this, but I do not think he was too surprised based on Manny's reputation. The project thus had to be modified. On my return to NYC Rudy told me to just do my job and do not worry about Manny. I was now no longer in good graces with Manny, and we rarely got together again. Not a terrific way to start my new job! The thought that ran through my mind was the line from

The Godfather where Abe Vigoda's "Salvatore Tessio" says to Robert Duvall's "Tom Hagen," "Tell Mike it was only business."

Within a few weeks of joining Westvaco, I was informed that the Corrugated Container division's HQ was going to be relocated to North Charleston, SC where the primary paper mill that supplied the paper to the corrugating plants was based. The target date would be in the summer, in time for the kids to start at new schools. I broke the news to Linda, and it took time for the color to come back to her face. We broke the news to the girls, now 7 and 4, and they took it well. The very mention of being near the beaches helped a lot.

So, in August, off we went. Westvaco bought our NJ townhouse, and we found a nice big (for us) house in Charleston's West Ashley neighborhood across the street from the Charleston Jewish Community Center. A pool, summer camps, and making lots of friends was icing on the cake. We moved in during August of 1988. I continued my travels to the corrugated container plants, so nothing changed in that respect other than now having easy access to Charleston International Airport. Coming "home" was so much nicer than arriving in snow-bound Newark Int'l airport.

33
THE LOW COUNTRY

Charleston, SC is indeed a beautiful city with family-friendly surrounding areas. The winters are usually mild although the summer heat and humidity can take one's breath away. There are, however, exceptions and within our first two years we encountered them.

South Carolina's summer weather in 1989 was normal with hot days and 3:00 pm thunderstorms. Weather forecasters were beginning to sound alarms about a hurricane heading toward us. Nothing so drastic had happened in recent memory and as such, weather bulletins were not taken too seriously. That was a mistake.

Hurricane Hugo arrived just before midnight on 9/21/88 with 140mph winds and a 40mph forward speed. It was like a spinning bowling ball. Heavy rain and high winds caused massive tree damage and downed power lines. We remained in the house during the storm as there were no evacuation warnings at the time. The girls slept in the upstairs foyer while Linda and I had visions of "Dorothy" in the Wizard of Oz. We sustained about $10,000 in structural damage but we were not hurt. Take a note: pay heed to hurricane warnings!

The largest snowstorm in history for the Southeast U.S. coast occurred in December 1989. We received eight inches of snow but due to the lack of equipment to clear roads for days it remained. I do recall seeing the most ingenious rendition of a snowplow. There were three men in a South Carolina DOT Chevy S10 pickup. There was the driver, his coworker, and a man in the bed of the pickup. The driver slowly drove as the co-worker in the passenger seat held a long-handled shovel out the window and "plowed" the streets. The man in the bed shoveled sand onto the road. It was what it was.

It was school break time. Linda was working as a hospital clerk and could not get time off to travel, so, I drove the kids to my mother's place in Lauderhill, FL for a few days for Grandma Rhoda to spoil them.

On the trip back all was going well until I passed a speed trap on US 17 about 30 min from home. I was pulled over and ticketed. I made the kids promise not to tell mom. That worked for like 10 minutes after we got home. I opted to go to "court" to see if I could plead to a lesser charge and save some money. The 'courthouse" was a mobile home in a rural area. The Judge appeared in sport clothes and summoned me to join him at his "bench," which was a card table. The police officer that cited me was present and sat nearby expressionless. The Judge said, "Yawl's got a ticket, boy?" He looked at the citation and again, in perfect diction said, "The officer says you were driving 80-mile an hour." He took out the law book, flipped to a well-used section, ran his finger down the page and showed me where it said he could fine me $250 (or so) BUT as he noted that I had no prior speeding citations, he let me off the hook for $100 but admonished me that "if I ever...!"

Ah yes - southern justice and again, memories of first-year English.

34
CHILDREN

OK, so by now you are asking, am I so self-absorbed with work so as not to give more space and detail here about the other two loves of my life, my children, Melanie Joy & Amy Lynne. My girls are on my mind 24/7. They may not know or always appreciate this but since their first breaths every decision I ever made was with their interests in mind. My girls are incredibly special in their own way. Each has a unique personality and during their formative years I shared more fun experiences with them that I could ever have imagined. I suppose genetics from past generations had a lot to do with this but suffice to say, it was always – and still is - a roller coaster ride of thrills, excitement, and delight.

They differ as much as night and day. Melanie was born into the center of attention. For her first three years, it was all her world. Then, when Amy arrived on scene, an unfamiliar word had to be learned - share!

Melanie was born to be cuddled and coddled. Amy was born to run. Jealousy for Melanie was an understatement. Mother nature: however, is a tough cookie and Melanie's occasional flare ups at her sister were sometimes met with brute force. Of course, Amy was content to be herself and defend her turf but all too often her big sister would be heard yelling "daaaaaady, she hit me"! We all knew which one was the instigator but a few scolds and a few hugs and kisses and other distractions was the normal response. We are talking at this stage over many years ago. Funny how little has changed. I am still; however, into the hugs of course for both.

As they grew up, they made BFFL's (yes, see...I learned the lingo), and it is great they still maintain some of those early friendships. Both girls developed wonderful habits. They somehow intuitively knew how to study (I missed that generational connection), did well in school and had numerous extracurricular activities that really added to their good character. What did I know about raising girls? Not a lot - I must thank Linda and her (late) mom, Diane (AKA Nana) for that. I was there to read bedtime stories in character voices, have my finger and toenails painted, makeup applied and when napping, get my hair cut, chaperone school tips etc. They grew up FAST!

Segue a bit to the school chaperone! My girls & I to this day vividly recall those iconic moments. Please allow me to share these gems.

The girls attended Orange Grove Elementary school in Charleston, SC. It was, and for sure, still is a wonderful school staffed by caring educators. Third-grade classes were given the honor of a field trip via the school bus to the Riverbanks Zoo, about 2 hours northwest of Columbia SC. I volunteered to chaperone the boys. At the average age of eight, many boys had what was referred to as attention deficit disorder (back in MY day, it was just unruly kids).

One of the boys (name withheld for his privacy should he read this) was a "poster boy" for attention deficit disorder. He was a sweet kid, but he would interfere continually, taunt classmates, you know, just being a royal pain in the neck who just would not listen. One of the zoo's attractions was the lion exhibit. A few docile lions were calmly sunning themselves in their space. There were at least three layers of fencing between them and the public which provided quite a good safety margin. The kid was really running amuck, so I held him up and told him if he did not behave, I would feed him to the lions. Of course, it was in jest so, do not get the notion I was at all serious. I KNOW in hindsight this was wrong and I am to this day sorry for doing it (but it worked). Hopefully that young man today is leading a successful life with no scars from that trip.

Fast forward three years later and yours truly once again was chaperone for the boys in Amy's third grade class. This trip went smoothly without incident as referenced above. Now, in fairness I must admit that I was never a stickler to rules (like you did not surmise that already). The teachers in charge of the trip (all female) included the assistant principal. They did not want the kids to eat anything and that included no ice cream. I am sorry. It was late spring, and the South Carolina heat and humidity was brutal. That was a cruel rule as the kids all looked wilted. So, I made them promise not to tell if…….! Great – a solemn pact was reached, and they kept their word but chocolate evidence on the faces and clothing, well, you know. The assistant principal was not happy and asked that rhetorical question of them "Did you have ice cream?" They all fibbed and said no but at their tender age, no one was arrested. My stock rose!

When my girls' time came for college, which was hard on me not seeing them regularly and/or being there to keep them safe from what they did not yet know about life, not surprisingly they did quite well. Now thus far you can gather I gush a lot about my kids, but since this is MY autobiography, it is only fair that I get to have some fun at their expense, right? OK girls. I will not......Oh, heck, just a couple, ok?

Teenagers are born to party. Parents are there to set the rules. Linda & I were on a vacation trip without the girls who were certainly old enough to fend for themselves for a few days especially with friends and their parents nearby as might be needed. Almost any parent would just before leaving say NO PARTIES IN THE HOUSE! Upon our arrival home we were pleased to see that all the furniture was still intact, carpets were not stained and there were no holes in the walls. We were proud of them – except for the huge plastic trash bag of empty beer and wine bottles (bought by whom???) which they inadvertently had left in front of the den fireplace. Either one or the other thought the other was to take it to the trash. Oh well. No actual harm done, just some embarrassment on their part in front of the 'rents. We let them live.

While Melanie was in the sorority house at UMass, her housemates had some fun talking about some of their childhood experiences and Melanie related how I used to read her stories and make animal sounds for fun. One of the "sounds" I used to pretend was that of a turtle and Melanie related that sound to her housemates. Melanie was moved to tears when they revealed the truth that turtles do NOT make sounds. Around midnight I received a call at home and all I heard was her screaming daaaaaaaaady! So sorry baby!

Upon graduating UMass, Melanie moved to the Boston area to start her career. As with me in my youth, she lived in a small place and pinched pennies (except with American Express). I drove up to check on her and realized that the old Camry we gave her at college was on its last err, ah…wheels. So, I took her for a ride to look at some "furniture" and saw her face light up when she realized Honda was a car brand and not a sofa. So, we picked out a used Accord and I made an agreement with her that since she was working. I would make the car payments if she took care of insurance and all gas and maintenance. She gushed and was moved to tears of gratitude. A few months later, she called to tell me the check engine light was on, but one of her "learned" college friends said it was only an "idiot light" and not to worry. Umm, no! I re-explained our deal, and she agreed to take it in. I was advised the repair cost was $600. Sensing a need to help, I attempted to offer it, but she said no, it is OK dad – I paid for it - but I hate spending $600 on something I cannot wear!!!! To my son-in-law Matt, who now knows her very well, I wish you luck lol!

Oh, just a couple more anecdotes.

Melanie somehow inherited my warped sense of humor and usually caught me off-guard every April 1 with some sort of prank. On one occasion she called me, crying that her apartment was burglarized and ransacked. I was ready to call the police when she said April fool. Yes, she 'got me" but her short-term memory came back to bite her. I enlisted Mel's boss at the Boston Public Library to see if there was a rush job she needed Melanie to work on over the next weekend. She loved the plan. Her boss beamed with a big yes! Matt would convince Mel that they needed to fly to Tampa and help his mom following her minor surgery. Poor Mel had a dilemma now to either go with her husband to aid his mom or stay home and work!! She called me practically in tears over what to do. I suggested she wait two days and then decide.

Two days later I set up a conference call with her boss and Matt (in the silence of course) with Melanie and I on the phone I then asked what she decided to do. With a teary "I don't know what to do dad," I said do not do either - which was followed in unison by all on the call with APRIL FOOL. My goodness - she sure did learn the use of those certain nasty words! Again, sorry baby - Dad's still RULE.

Amy of course was never the troublemaker (ahem,) and was very friendly in all aspects. In high school she was a member of BBYO, the Jewish organization for girls (B'nai B'rith Youth Organization), and on occasional weekends they had sleepouts at a Jewish Community Center. Alcoholic beverages were somehow snuck in (imagine that!!!) and long story short, the kids were caught, and their parents were notified to get them. Linda & I were in Aruba and Amy was staying a few days with a neighbor/friend so that the mom picked them up. When we got home the truth was revealed. I grounded her with a 2-week hiatus from computer use (that lasted a couple of days).

My girls are now fully grown, beautiful, and in full control of their lives. Nothing could make Linda and me prouder of them. Melanie is married to Matt Camp, and they have given us two beautiful grandkids.

Grandson Dylan is seven going on fifteen and granddaughter Cece is four and I am trying to keep her that young.

Amy is married to Glenn Wright and in keeping with the tradition, presented us with grandson number three, Kessler, now 16 months old. My sons-in-law are great guys and treat my girls just as they so deserve.

35
THE BRUTAL TRUTH

The first order of business for a Safety Manager is to look at injury records and plant conditions. My work was cut out when I learned that this corrugated container division had the worst OSHA statistical record of recordable injuries. This is an issue that should never be taken lightly. Aside from potentially high OSHA fines for safety violations, possible criminal indictments, lost revenue due to reduced production, injuries and/or damage, there is also a morale issue. Hourly employees work extremely hard at their jobs and at times there is friction between what they vs. management see as "problems." It was not hard for me to see through the issues. Here are some examples:

When I returned from a non-union southern plant, the facility's General Manager called me in Charleston and wasted no time in berating and accusing me of stirring up trouble. For whatever reason, to my thinking, he did not have a good cadre of supervision and many of the plant's labor-saving devices were either broken or just neglected. It was no wonder to me why there were so many back injuries. Being still a new employee, I did not want to again create friction, so I approached his boss, the Regional Manager who gave me sound advice. He said to just do my job and get my love at home. Great advice!

Of course, I had the authority to visit anytime I wanted but out of respect for his position I made a peace offering.

I would work with maintenance, empower some employees to direct needed repairs and within a year he would have the BEST safety record in the entire company. Subsequent visits were a lot different. Male and female hourly employees (who were not spring chickens) were coming up to me to thank me and asking what I did to effect such profound changes!

The answer was empowerment and teamwork. The plant was a lot cleaner, much more efficient, and free of the back injuries that had been a problem. By the end of the year the injury rate dropped to near zero. The GM thanked me, and I really felt good about what was accomplished.

At another plant (this one being a union shop) I was "summoned" to the production floor to offer my opinion on what was indeed a huge safety issue. The machine in question produced large wardrobe boxes used in household moves. Flat corrugated boards were manually pushed forward by an operator seated within a cut out notch on a hydraulic lift table. In this instance, a lynch pin failed, and the hydraulic table tilted down at a steep angle. The operator was fine as his seated position was out of harm's way.

Maintenance replaced the table but without a notched area. They simply removed some rollers and placed the operator in position except that now there was a rear steel border of the table across his back. If the lynchpin failed again, he would be seriously hurt. So, there I was facing the operator, bystander employees, the Production Manager, and the union steward. I was asked if I considered this "fix" safe. I said no. Smiles from all emerged except the Production Manager who stormed off in a huff into his office and shut the door. I shut down the machine (on my authority) until it would be put back in the correct condition and then walked into the Production Manager's office.

The poor guy was furious. The plant was losing revenue and a lot was riding on his shoulders. I told him that may be true, but my question is would you put your son in that jury-rigged contraption? He breathed a sigh and said no. I said, well then, go out there and apologize to that worker. In fact, I will go with you! He did not want to but did. His "stock" went up and harmony reigned. I added psychologist to my job description.

While conducting a safety survey at another union shop, I noted a lift truck parked under an overhead pipe that pneumatically moved paper scrap from machinery to designated scrap collection rooms. An employee was in a cage attached to the forks of the lift truck and was elevated about thirty feet up to the pipe where he needed to clear a jam through a clean-out access port. The driver was behind the wheel, and a third employee was a spotter to keep people and equipment at a safe distance.

Then I about froze when I saw the man in the cage climb out of it and straddle the side of the cage to reach the pipe. He was not wearing a safety harness and thus was in direct violation of OSHA standards, let alone that he would be killed if he fell. He saw me, climbed back into the cage, and the cage was lowered to the floor. I approached them and, with smiles, that previously elevated employee said, "Hey college boy …what's new?" My reply changed his attitude and his skin tone. I said "Oh, nothing but the next time you go up in a cage, with or without a harness, you might want to check that the cage is chained and secured to the mast. Have a lovely day, boys." Somehow, I did not think friction alone was a safe bet.

36
MOVIN' ON OUT

By the mid 1990's the girls were making lots of friends, enjoying school and we were all happy. Then, as before, company changes caused disruption. Weyerhaeuser Co. purchased the corrugated-container operations of Westvaco Corp. plants that I had "serviced" for 8 years. Weyerhaeuser Co. was based in Tacoma, WA and depending on how one looks at it as being bad or good, I was not invited.

After a few months of severance pay and uncertainty, I was asked if I would like to remain with Westvaco as the Safety Manager for their Envelope Manufacturing division, based in Springfield, MA. Not a lot of choice there. As much as we did not want to leave Charleston, job prospects there were not good locally and certainly I would not make near the money I had been making. So, with Melanie now a HS sophomore and Amy entering Middle school, an excellent job opportunity was not to be turned down. The kids; however, were disappointed.

As you know, from my childhood I had been there and done that, but the stigma is far worse for girls at 16 & 13. I felt awful. Linda was not pleased about a return to the northeast and there was not a darn thing I could do about it. So, in March 1996, I began working up there and commuting weekly from our Charleston home. The winter of 1996 in Springfield continued well into late March and I detested every minute of it. We purchased a home in Longmeadow, MA, just south of Springfield and we re-started the process of being newcomers. I will say that we did make many new friends and socially life was OK, but Linda and I never really accepted this as home.

37
Deja Vous

The process began at the Envelope Division as it did eight years prior at the Corrugated Division. There were twelve major envelope production plants plus some smaller locations and all need to be seen ASAP. I was very encouraged at first because I knew that the Envelope Division had an excellent safety record and in fact had won Westvaco Corp's coveted President's Award several years in a row. That was a ruse!

My first trip was to the San Francisco location. Winning an award is one thing. Earning it is another. Safety awards are based on a statistical OSHA formula that calculates the number of injuries (defined as where treatment beyond first aid is rendered) multiplied by a standard factor of 200,000 (representing one hundred employees working 50 weeks a year at 40 hours/week (100x50x40). This is then divided by the actual number of total hours worked for the year. For example, if a plant sustained five recorded injuries and worked 200,000 hours the incident rate would be five. That would be a respectable number, but the Envelope Division was reporting a rate of ZERO.

The only way to know the truth is to do what OSHA representatives would do if they visited a plant which would be to look at Federally required OSHA logs and do the math. What I found in San Francisco was the beginning and not an anomaly. I requested three years of OSHA logs be sent to me from each location and I found the truth. There was an inside "cover up" utilizing two "sets of books."

My boss was the Division's Manufacturing Manager. His predecessor was now a Plant Manager in the Midwest. When I revealed my findings to my boss, he knew that I just uncovered a major problem. I knew he knew about it. We talked and I said look, you hired me to do my job!

Fess up! I also had the backing of the Corporation. The prior awards were trashed, and my "welcome" at all plants was about to be a very rude awakening. Welcome to the next six years!

38
Fairness

Business is business. Humanity is another story – unless what one can do for another can and will improve their business. That was my job. I was able to develop trust and deliver on promises such as enhanced management and employee safety training programs, detailed inspections/surveys to demonstrate where plant improvements could be implemented and in general providing them the assistance that had been lacking for way too long. I met some of the most wonderful people at the local levels and I looked forward to helping where I could. One of my new "roles" was the managing of the Division's worker's compensation program which was administered by a third party.

When an employee reports an injury (or an occupational illness defined such as a repetitive motion trauma), it is imperative that it not only be promptly reported but that appropriate treatment is provided ASAP. An incident investigation then follows, and corrective actions and, if applicable, employee discipline may result. Worker's Comp coverage is not perfect and depending on the nature of the injury, it may not provide the employee with medical benefits as might be expected. This gap creates an opportunity for fraud. If (when) injured employees (on the job) are not awarded the benefits they believe they deserve, it then becomes a legal battle.

My employer was self-insured for up to $1 million. Profit was always critical and worker's comp payments strongly impacted the bottom line. My predecessor was originally a floor supervisor and was not too fond of believing an employee who claimed he or she was hurt on the job unless it was patently obvious. Thus, sometimes it was a matter of trust as to if an on-the-job injury really occurred or if it was faked to get benefits.

As coordinator for our third-party administration company, I did have some discretion in cases unless lawyers were in the mix. Low back injuries from either falls on the job or because of repeated trauma are indeed painful. Yes, I valued the judgment of our third-party administration, but I knew at times more than they did about some of the employees and on occasion, was able to get the needed medical benefits to the employee that had been denied on a basis of he said/she said and no real proof. I recall an older employee in the office was "on the books" as an injured employee and was receiving some medical benefits because of a slip and fall in front of a soft drink vending machine in the office building. For some reason, his benefits were cut off. I received a call from the man's wife who was distraught because of this monetary impact. I investigated and learned that someone from the third-party administrator arbitrarily cut the benefits because there was no formal proof that the claim was legitimate.

I personally was familiar with the location of the vending machine and had maintenance address complaints about soda or ice spillage on the tile floor. Drip pans were installed. The claim was made long prior to this action. I interjected and reopened the file and had the employee receive a check for the stopped benefits. His wife called in tears to thank me. Hey, you know, sometimes just doing the right thing is not overlooked.

Prior to being self-insured for $1 million, it was for $500,000. Long prior to me being in the job a maintenance employee had fallen from a roof and was paralyzed. He was appropriately awarded lifetime benefits for his care. Once the $500,000 self-insured limit was reached, a reinsurance company would pay the future costs.

Our third-party claims administration company would cut the checks on our behalf and then submit them to the reinsurance carrier for reimbursement. One day while reviewing a loss run report for the plant where this employee worked, I noted that we paid out over $750,000 in benefits. It turned out that someone messed up on resubmitting the excess of $500,000 to the reinsurance company. I got back into my boss' good graces a few weeks later when I handed him a check for over $250,000. He asked where I got it. I joked and said, "don't ask – just deposit it."

39
The End of the Corporate Risk Control Road

In early 2001 life was rolling along fine for us in Massachusetts. Linda was happily employed as a front office manager for an OBGYN practice, and I continued doing my risk control work for Westvaco's Envelope Division. Melanie was starting her sophomore year at the University of Massachusetts and Amy was entering her senior year at Longmeadow High School. Then the changes began once more.

Westvaco was merging with Mead Corporation and as a result, there were staff cutbacks announced. My termination was a bit of a surprise, but the company softened the monetary impact by providing six months of severance via the usual pay checks.

My first thought was financially caring for my family. Although I knew this was through no fault of my work, it was still a demoralizing blow. Westvaco provided outplacement services to assist those laid off in finding other jobs. Using all resources in my search for a job I spoke with an ex-coworker who had a lead on a risk control job with Lucent Technologies in NYC.

M&MPC had recently moved their midtown Manhattan offices to the World Trade Center, and I was invited to meet some people from Lucent the next week with some of the

M&MPC people there. I was advised the day before the meeting that it would be postponed and so I did not drive down to Queens and stay with my in-laws as I had planned to do the night before the meeting.

Instead, I left the house around 8am on Tuesday September 11, 2001, for a routine meeting with my outplacement counselor in Springfield, MA. I was listening to the syndicated NYC based Imus in the Morning radio show in the car when there was a report that an airplane crashed into the World Trade Center in lower Manhattan. At first it was not thought of as anything but an accident. At 8:46am American Airlines Flight 11 crashed at roughly 466 mph into the north face of the North Tower (1 WTC) of the World Trade Center, between floors 93 and 99.

The aircraft entered the tower intact and it plowed into the building's core, severing all three gypsum-encased stairwells, dragging combustibles with it. A powerful shock wave traveled down to the ground and up again. The combustibles and the remnants of the aircraft were all ignited by the burning fuel. As the building lacked a traditional full cage frame and depended entirely on the strength of a narrow structural core running up the center, fire at the center of the impact zone compromised the integrity of all internal columns and caused the building to collapse.

People below the severed stairwells started to evacuate, but no one above the impact zone was able to do so. Marsh & McLennan's offices were on the 102nd floor of 1 WTC. 295 employees and sixty-three consultants including those I worked with died. Then, at 9:03am United Airlines' Flight

175 crashed at about 590 mph into the south face of the South Tower (2 WTC) of the World Trade Center, between floors 77 and 85. All 65 people on board the aircraft died instantly on impact, and hundreds in the building as well. My job search was now a trivial matter. Nothing would ever be the same again.

I refocused my search to the world of insurance risk control consulting. Some insurance carriers did not have risk control staff, so they hired out on an hourly basis. I did this for about a year driving all over MA, CT, VT, and NH to conduct risk assessments and issue reports. The pay was low, but it helped!

40
CHANGING STRIPES, AGAIN

In mid-2002 I reached out to the Western MA chapter of the American Society of Safety Engineers and via their website looked at job postings. I connected with a recruiter for a job in Atlanta, GA with CNA Insurance. It looked promising but then I was advised that the job had just been filled. A day or so later the recruiter called saying the new hire changed his mind and that the Risk Control Manager saw my resume, knew me, and wanted to talk with me. That Risk Control Manager and I sat side by side at desks in Morristown with M&MPC over 20 years prior! Small world. He set me up with an interview with their Hartford, CT office, got a great report and asked me to come down to Atlanta to talk. He offered me the job and on January 3, 2003, we signed the closing papers on the Longmeadow house and moved to Georgia!

We rented a three-bedroom townhouse in Alpharetta, about twenty-five miles north of the City of Atlanta. We figured it would be best to learn the area and then decide where to buy a home. CNA's office was in Duluth, GA, a 30-minute drive from Alpharetta. Melanie had graduated from UMass and was now gainfully employed in Boston with the Boston Public Library associated with fundraising efforts and becoming a political insider. We were immensely proud of her (and of course, still are).

Amy had applied to the University of Florida, The University of GA and as a fall-back, UMass. She was accepted at each and chose UGA. She was in her second year when we moved to GA. That worked out well as she now had a local home to come to, and because we were now GA taxpayers, her tuition costs were almost cut in half to the in-state rate. CNA supplied me with a leased car for the job, so we gave Amy our 1996 Camry and bought a new Nissan Maxima for Linda. In the summer of 2004, Linda and I purchased a beautiful home in a residential neighborhood of Alpharetta GA.

Not long after moving into our new home, we met many nice neighbors and after a bit of being prodded, I was asked to join the board of the neighborhood's Homeowners' Association (HOA). Soon after, I was "drafted" to accept the job as the HOA Board President. I briefly self-debated this but received encouragement from Linda, who said I would do a fantastic job. This comment was also supported by Linda's sisters and my new friends, so I accepted the opportunity. The one person who I SHOULD have listened to, was my mother-in-law, Diane, who succinctly stated, "Schmuck...... they could not find anyone else? Thanks Ma! I stayed on that HOA post for 5 years.

The insurance job was going fine. I adjusted to the insurance risk control side quickly. I had now come full circle from AIG to M&MPC to City Investing, Westvaco and now to CNA. After over 13 years in the corporate risk control arena, I realized that although the surveys were similar there was an enormous difference. In the corporate role my job was to help the company avoid costly losses through improved practices and to a lesser extent, keep management from making bad decisions that would result in heavy fines from regulatory agencies – and to keep some of them out of jail! The insurance work was slightly different as I needed to convince underwriters to avoid underwriting poor risks that would cost CNA money to pay the incurred losses. Occasionally that did not work out too well. In the insurance world there is a saying that goes "don't let the perfume of the premium permeate the stench of the risk." Eventually some got the message.

41
REALITY

An insurance company underwriter's annual performance is measured on several financially tied factors. A major goal is the number of premium dollars written. Most are not remunerated on a commission basis. Doing as such would be folly. Bonuses: however, are often paid if the underwriting premium goal is met and/or exceeded. A takeaway is the loss ratio loosely defined as how much money has been paid out in claims vs. the premium collected. Whereas underwriting management may also utilize various mathematical algorithms to narrow the risk margin, this is quite different from an exact science.

The risk control representative's input is intended to advise the underwriter of the identified potential loss-producing factors and to provide recommendations to mitigate the loss potential. Risk control representatives utilize existing Federal and/or State regulations such as OSHA & EPA standards, and National Fire Protection Assn. codes and Federal Motor Carrier Safety Assn. (FMCSA) records. Depending on the seriousness or the volume of non-compliant items, a risk control rep may simply not recommend a line of coverage. If the underwriter choses to downplay or worse, ignore the risk control input, the likelihood of a costly loss to the insurance company goes up. Here is an example of one of my business confrontations at CNA:

In 2004, I attended a training seminar at CNA's Duluth GA office which was provided to all CNA risk control employees and underwriters. The speaker was a senior manager out of the Chicago office. He was addressing the underwriting limitations for auto liability. He mentioned that risk control employees should always say not recommended if the risk is not conducting their own in-house driver history via the motor vehicle records (MVRs). I nudged my coworker and quietly said "like that is ever going to happen!" Clever idea for sure but they rely on the insurance carrier to do this for them – and the carrier does it for its own purpose. An insured would be foolish to allow an employee to drive a company (or rented) vehicle where the employee had received speeding tickets, or worse. The speaker overheard my whispered comment and mentioned it to the Duluth office's Senior Manager who in turn mentioned it to my boss. I was summoned into my boss's office the next day where he related to me what I said and that made the Senior Manager angry. Well by now you may have surmised that on occasion I do stand my ground, so I suggested we visit the Senior Manager and address this issue. Further, I asked him if he really wanted us to not recommend every auto-liability risk that does not do their own employee's MVR checks."

He declined my request that we see the Senior Manager and he also agreed that we never use that criterion alone for not recommending a risk to underwriting. I "politely" told him to never use me as a pawn and that I do not hide from the truth, and neither should he (spineless SOB).

42
KEEP CLIMBING

In 2005 I received a call from a recruiter about a risk control job with Westfield Insurance, an Ohio-based carrier needing a risk control rep in Duluth, GA and would I be interested. Yes! Whereas I did have a wonderful job with CNA, pay raises and annual bonuses were extremely low. I needed a change. I had a brief talk with the recruiter and was advised that Westfield management wanted to meet with me in their Ohio office.

Westfield's corporate office and grounds are like a well-manicured college campus complete with a championship golf course. There are also about 1200 people all working together as if this was Santa's workshop. I was ushered into the main building's rotunda to meet the top three managers for the Risk Control department, and we sat in a nice well-appointed conference room for a group interview. I was then required to take a written skills set exam. I always disliked taking these tests because I did not think they really showed the true talent of the individual. I did OK (although I was never told this).

Following the interview and the exam I was invited to join them all for lunch in the cafeteria and meet some of the other department heads. It was an incredibly positive experience. We wrapped up discussion and I was advised I would hear from them shortly via the recruiter on a decision as they were also talking with other candidates. I was picked up at the main entrance by one of the company's shuttle buses for the ride back to the Akron/Canton airport. If I had any doubt as to how it all went such thinking was rapidly dispelled when the driver said, "well it looks like you did well." I asked why he thought so. He further stated that "They wouldn't have taken you to lunch if you didn't pass muster and they would have put you on an earlier shuttle had they not liked you." This was a remarkably interesting perspective and as it turned out, he was 100% correct.

I received a call the next day from the recruiter that Westfield was offering me the job and did not want to take no for an answer. The salary was about the same as I was making with CNA but the massive surprise -and draw-was a bonus structure that was off the charts. The prior year ALL employees received an annual bonus equal to 70% of their base pay. As the late great NY Yankees broadcaster Mel Allen used to say, "How about that!? I accepted the employment offer.

After formally resigning from CNA with questions from management as to why (although they knew they could not compete financially), I took a few days off and then went back to Ohio for some orientation and training. Over dinner I asked my boss why they hired me. He said, "We interviewed seven people and you were the only one with the right personality plus a genuine pair of balls." Hey, that works for me!

Risk control representatives and underwriters do usually work well together, although the inevitable friction surfaces when the underwriter feels that the risk control representative is being too strict and thus it becomes difficult for them to underwrite what they had worked on and hoped would be a good account – and thus add to their underwriting goals. My nickname became Dr. No. This was especially true with auto liability coverage for trucking companies that had poor FMCSA historical scores. Westfield eventually (and wisely) dropped this line of business.

If you do not mind, I will toot my horn here (pardon the pun) just a bit. My boss (Dave) came down to ATL from Ohio and wanted to accompany me to a potential client that was a general building construction contractor. Conducting the risk control survey was easy for me as I had honed some good methods with CNA. At the conclusion of the survey, we got back in the car to leave, and he said he'd, "never seen that before!" I said, "Never seen what?" He said, "your methods were so smooth that it was more like a regular conversation vs. an inquisition as is so common with most risk control representatives and you covered everything!" Another Mel Allen moment, go ahead, "How about that?!"

I met so many wonderful people in this job and looked forward to the daily challenges that lay ahead. Inevitable confrontations arose now and then, but most often, they were a pleasant experience. Some, in fact, to me, were humorous. Here are some examples:

While attending a "Meet & Greet" party of risk control and underwriters I was tapped on my elbow by the President of the Commercial Lines underwriting dept. This woman overheard me chatting and asked, "Did I really think that what underwriting does is basically legalized gambling?" With respect to her position, I politely asked her if the company spends a lot of time and resources on defining which types of risks would provide maximum profit and low loss ratios, isn't that right?" She said, 'Well yes we do, Steve." I then asked if she could tell me when the next loss might occur." She said "Of course not." I replied. "That's my point." Call it what you want but it is akin to handicapping or in other words playing the odds – which is gambling. My role, if you will, is as the handicapper. She slowly walked away. Why is it so difficult for executives to recognize basic concepts?

I received a call from a senior underwriter in Pennsylvania whose job was to approve or deny renewals on certain risk classes, depending on performance history. I was the insurance carrier's risk control representative for a large underground utility contractor in Georgia. I worked with this account for many years and this company had an exemplary safety record with very few losses. In fact, on my advice, they also instituted a program to return any injured employee back to work in a light duty capacity (per medical approval) thus reducing potential worker's compensation payments.

The underwriter was upset because the risk failed to provide light duty to an employee who sustained a low-back injury on the job and the accumulated indemnity payments were approaching $60,000. This injured employee could not return to a light duty assignment per doctor's orders and as such began collecting worker's compensation indemnity payments.

Because of this the underwriter wanted to cancel the renewal. I objected but did so in a unique manner.

I asked the underwriter if he has ever played Blackjack at a casino. The answer was yes. I then laid out a scenario and asked him to follow along. He said OK. I said, "You sit down at the table with a stake of $200 in casino chips and the ante before cards are dealt is $10." He said "OK." "I said "You get dealt a pair of eights. What will you do?" He said, "I'd split them." I said, "Good move and you now need to put up an additional $10 for the next two cards." He said "OK." I said, "This means so far you have now invested 10% of your stake on the first hand." He said "OK." I said "One card is then dealt to each of the eights and the dealer is showing a face card value of 4. The two additional cards are threes. Do you want to double down on each of the 8/3 combos? Doing so means a total of $40 or 20% of your stake on this firsthand but your odds are good that you will win at least on one of the hands or maybe both but then again you could also lose both." He said, "It depends how I feel at the time." I said "Listen, you have collected almost $2 million in premium from this risk, and you want to cancel based on this ONLY loss reaching maybe $60K?" I said "Do us a favor and leave the table, take your casino chips to the cashier, cash out, go home and just renew this account. Do the math!" He agreed and renewed the account. Did I mention psychology was part of my skill set?

43
A (NOT SO) LUCKY BREAK

In July 2009 I was home and working on a risk control report and lamenting how many more hours a day or week I must do this work. It was just a thought, but I may as well have rubbed an old lamp and let out a genie. As our neighborhood's HOA President, I received a call from a contractor working at our pool clubhouse. The contractor needed access to a utility closet, and I had the keys. So, I backed away from the computer and walked over to the clubhouse to open the locked door. On my return I noticed a Federal Express delivery truck coming down my street toward the stop sign at the main road I was crossing. I gave a short-wave hello, but the driver simply looked to his right, did not stop at the stop sign and turned left onto the main road and directly into me. I was struck full on, knocked backward onto the asphalt, and realized I had been a lot better a few minutes ago at my computer, but since I asked how much longer I wanted to do this, this was the Almighty's answer.

I recall instinctively rolling onto my side and onto the grassy curb area. My first thought other than the pain in many places, was I sure hope I am not lying in a fire ant nest! The driver stopped, got out and asked if I was OK. I said, "No" but my thinking was "Just fine you asshole." Being July, the pool was full of moms and kids, and I vaguely saw numerous cell phones calling 911.

In a moment, the City of Milton dispatched an ambulance, a fire truck, and a police car. I had my cell phone in my pocket and managed to call Linda at her office. I did not reveal too much other than I was hit by a FedEx truck while walking. In retrospect I am sure she freaked out but had the presence of mind to come home quickly. One of the two police officers intercepted her at the main entrance and escorted her to where the EMT's were prepping me for the ride to the hospital. She came along. I did not fully realize it, but my left wrist was shattered, my left shoulder rotator tendon was torn, and I had a fractured vertebra. Three surgeries later plus a gallbladder removal based on unrelated matters that just added to the fun sidelined me for 6 months on disability. The two police officers came by a few days later to investigate and ask me if the driver ever stopped.

I said no. One of the officers then mentioned I looked familiar to him. Turns out he had been in a landscape business with his brother, and I had performed the insurance risk control survey. He came by again about two weeks later while I was in never-never land on opioids. Linda greeted him at the door. He said he just wanted to know how I was doing. How many local police officers do you know that do that??? I sent an email to the police chief commending this officer on his caring act. A few months later I saw that officer at our local gas station while we were each refueling. He remembered me and thanked me for the letter to the chief which resulted in an accommodation for him. Note to self - always appreciate the service of someone else!

I am OK today although there are some minor physical limitations that I can and will live with. A legal claim was instituted, and we settled out of court about a year later (for an undisclosed amount). Somehow the expression of" being thrown under the bus" has new meaning. I do not recommend it.

A year later, Linda was experiencing back pain that was getting worse. She was evaluated and was informed that a spinal fusion was her only option. Thankfully that procedure in 2011 worked well and after a few months of therapy and hard recovery work, she began to resume a pain-free life. Following the surgery, she was informed that her "services" were no longer required at her new office job as they did not want to spend time on training her with any limitations she may have. Perhaps this was an illegal employment action, but I had a better idea.

We were able to live OK on my income and I wanted nothing more than her just taking it easy. She was convinced that I was right, and soon after, she discovered a white 2006 BMW with a black convertible top parked in our driveway. She looked awesome in her "dream car" and found it perfectly OK to drive about and resume her tennis-playing passion. Although I was sufficiently recovered from the FedEx accident, she still kicked my butt on the courts! I remained at Westfield just over 9 years when I decided that it was time to make my preparations to retire.

44
WEDDING TIME

During their beautiful courtship, Matt called me while Linda and I were attending an Atlanta Braves baseball game to ask for our blessing for him to propose marriage to Melanie. Kidding of course, I said are you SURE? (of course, I said yes). The storybook wedding took place on the island of Jamaica on May 26, 2012.

The Island of Jamaica indeed is a beautiful locale for a wedding. The ceremony was on the beach at Couples Negril. with the blue Caribbean Sea water as the backdrop, Melanie indeed stood out as a gorgeous bride (oh, come on – I can gush if I want to) and her handsome beau, Matt, was as doting as can be and still is!

Mom Linda, of course, drew raves! The dinner party was great, and the speeches were fun. Of course, Melanie's (now ex) boss from the Boston Public Library attended and I just HAD to restate that April Fool's story just to humble the stunning bride! After dinner, it was party time at a piano bar with lots of alcohol and dancing. The piano player was very talented, and as he played, Nana Diane sang her heart out and they entertained everyone with duets. What a hoot! We were all so thrilled she was able to make the trip!

45
Turning a Corner

In 2013, at the suggestion of many friends, I joined the age 55-year-plus North Atlanta Men's Club comprised of many like-minded senior men and began to enjoy plenty of fun activities to keep me mostly out of trouble. Although I had neither any long-term plans, nor commitments. as the old saying goes, "One doesn't stop playing because they get old - they get old because they stop playing." Life was great!

I was pleased to serve on the Club's Board positions starting as Camaraderie Coordinator for member activities for two years and then as the Club's VP for another two years. In 2019, I was nominated to take on the role as President of the Club, now with a membership of over two hundred men. At the December 2019 annual breakfast meeting I began my term as the new Board President. I stood at the podium and related my tale of woe as an HOA President and related my mother-in-law Diane's quip. A raucous laughter followed, and my title was now unofficially "President Schmuck." Great guys!!!! Will I EVER learn?

On 2/23/2013 I turned sixty-seven, and Linda would be sixty-five on 3/1/2014, and both of us would then be eligible to receive Social Security and Medicare benefits. Given our financial status with pending pensions, the Fed-Ex settlement, and an IRA investment portfolio, I opted to leave the rat race 3/1/2014. It has now been eight years since I retired.

46
WEDDING PART DEUX

Our, not so long ago, little Amy had been dating Glenn Wright in the DC-area and following the time-honored tradition, I again was asked to give a daughter's hand in marriage. Linda and I were thrilled and once again, plans were underway for a wedding ceremony and reception. The kids opted to have it on a Virgina farm with the wedding venue being a converted old barn. It was indeed a beautiful place. Although not Jewish, Glenn was insistent on a traditional Jewish ceremony including a Chuppah (a wedding canopy used in Jewish weddings where the bride, groom, and whoever is officiating (and sometimes both sets of parents) stand under during the wedding ceremony.) Being a great craftsman, he and a friend built and transported the Chuppah to the farm. Glenn was also excited to conduct The Breaking of the Glass which symbolizes the destruction of the Jewish temple in Jerusalem. Couples include this tradition in their wedding ceremony as it symbolizes the absolute finality of the marital covenant. Just as the broken pieces of glass can never be put back together and returned to their former state, so the covenant of marriage irrevocably binds the new husband and wife in their new state of marriage. Following the marital ceremony, I once again had the honor of making the "Dad's speech" as I did 7 years prior in Jamaica, and I reflected on Amy growing up through the years.

Of course, Glenn knows her well, and I could not help but express my appreciation for him honoring the traditional Jewish marital ceremony, but with one slight twist. While I stated that I really did not know the long history of breaking the glass, I did say that that was the last opportunity of a husband of a Jewish wife to ever put his foot down hard again! The ensuing laughter rattled the barn!

47
LIVING WITH FEAR

In March 2019 Linda & I again enjoyed our spring vacation on the island of Aruba as we discussed Amy & Glenn's pending wedding. Little did we know that Covid-19 was about to rule the world. As we sat on the beach under our palapa and the ever-present Caribbean breezes (and Pina Coladas) refreshed us, the thought occurred to me that we are in an incubator with thousands of world travelers arriving daily from areas already reporting high infection rates.

Further, the thought of flying back to Atlanta in a large and crowded Delta jet was not going to be without serious health risks. There were no mask mandates yet nor any vaccinations yet available. Once home we became self-quarantined, and our lifestyle became reclusive and fearful. Eventually we both tested (negative) for Covid-19, and we did receive our two vaccinations in February 2021 and December (2021) and two subsequent boosters. As everyone on the planet soon knew, the Covid -19 pandemic was – and remains – a dreadful and formidable foe. Listening to scientists, pundits, newscasters, social media outlets et.al, just added more chaos and confusion and altered humanity as never before.

As each year brings new and exciting changes, 2021 was just a bit more special as Amy & Glenn introduced us to their first child and now our second grandson, Kessler Elliot Damsker-Wright.

With Grammy Linda and Grampa Steve now just loving life, we continue with our involvements in local social activities and travel frequently to Boston and to DC to see our children and the grandchildren, or their families come here, and all turn our Georgia home into the chaos we recall from the days when our girls were little. The Camp kids are Dylan, seven, and Cecelia ("Cece"), four and with the new little guy, Kessler, now 16 months, spoiling our grandkids as often as possible makes life great!

CPSIA information can be obtained
at www.ICGtesting.com
Printed in the USA
JSHW021744180922
30572JS00001B/24

9 798218 073176